"With honesty and optimism this book biblically equips step-families to overcome the weeds that threaten healthy stepfamily growth. Kay has written a very useful tool for your relational toolbox."

—Ron L. Deal, author and director, SuccessfulStepfamilies.com

"How refreshing to find a book that addresses so many sensitive issues of stepparenting! Having 'been there and done that,' Kay presents steps for stepparents that are both practical and poignant. For anyone considering a second marriage where children are present and sometimes problematic, this book is a must read."

—June Hunt, Hope for the Heart Ministries

"A must read for all partners in a blended family! Kay is careful to quote statistics—meaningful but not overwhelming. She uses descriptive words to help you feel the emotions expressed on paper. As she identifies specific issues and challenges, she provides practical helps born out of personal experience, careful research, and bibilical principles. Each chapter provides interactive activities causing the reader to think about his or her own beliefs and experiences. Kay Adkins writes in an honest and transparent manner. She shares with her readers her own shortcomings, allowing them to see her as a real person rather than a theorist/researcher."

—Marcia McQuitty, associate professor of childhood education,
Southwestern Baptist Theological Seminary

"I am only too happy to commend Kay Adkins's book *I'm Not Your Kid*. It is a well-researched and sensitive book filled with practical advice to help stepfamilies succeed. I especially like her section on 'Why Stepfamilies Can't Go Nuclear,' where she calls stepfamilies 'tectonic families.' Such an apt description. Congratulations on an excellent book."

—Dick Dunn, author of *New Faces in the Frame*

"Few resources are available to help stepfamilies make their way in today's world. Kay Adkins opens the door to her own home and shares from her personal experience, taking the reader on a journey that shows both the difficulties and the possible triumphs of stepfamily life. With each chapter, readers will discover accurate descriptions of life in a stepfamily as well as practical suggestions for achieving family health and strength. Most of all, however, readers will find hope for traversing the difficult terrain of stepfamily life. I recommend this book for counselors, educators, ministers, and anyone who is a part of life in a stepfamily."

—Scott Floyd, associate professor of counseling and psychology,
Southwestern Baptist Theological Seminary

I'm *Not* Your Kid

A Christian's Guide
to a Healthy *Stepfamily*

KAY ADKINS

Baker Books

A Division of Baker Book House Co
Grand Rapids, Michigan 49516

Published by Baker Books
a division of Baker Book House Company
P.O. Box 6287, Grand Rapids, MI 49516-6287
www.bakerbooks.com

Printed in the United States of America

Library of Congress Cataloging-in-Publication Data
Adkins, Kay, 1960-
    I'm not your kid : a Christian's guide to a healthy stepfamily / Kay Adkins.
       p.   cm.
    Includes bibliographical references.
    ISBN 0-8010-6461-9 (pbk.)
    1. Family—Religious aspects—Christianity. 2. Stepfamilies—Religious life.
  I. Title.
  BT707.7.A35 2004
  248.4—dc22   2003024252

To
the Redeemer of lives and Rebuilder of families,
the Lord Jesus Christ;
my husband, Carl, who supports me on the journey;
my stepdaughters, Melissa and Tracy;
and to stepfamilies everywhere who need
an abundance of God's grace

Contents

Preface

(Na, na, na, na, na)
My stepkids ignore me. (Na, na, na, na, na)
They think I'm uncool. (Na, na, na, na, na)
My life's unrewarding.
I'm buried in a pit,
I've got the Blended Family Blues . . .
Oh, yeah!
I've got the Blended Family Blues.

C an you sing this with me? Can you hear it in your head? Then you've probably been there yourself. If not, perhaps you want to avoid getting the stepfamily blues, or you know someone currently buried in that pit, someone who needs a helping hand.

Stepfamily life is a unique experience for which couples who remarry don't usually prepare. The relationship challenges that arise can overwhelm blended families, and believing "I deserve better than this" does little to see them through the tough times. The blues we succumb to keep us focused on ourselves, to the destruction of our families. Sometimes we need a jolt of reality to get out of our self-pity and back on the road to becoming what stepfamilies can be: strong, responsible agents of grace for all who might have been damaged by divorce or other kinds of harmful relationships.

I'm Not Your Kid is intended as a tool to provide that jolt of reality. Divorced people preparing for remarriage, remarried adults in stepfamilies, pastors, and family counselors (either lay counselors or professionals) can get a better idea of the challenges unique to stepfamily life and how to make the best of this complex situation.

While the Bible doesn't contain a specific book on how to make it as a stepfamily, God still has a plan. Stepfamilies with a clear vision of the possibilities and a commitment to work toward God's dream in God's way will see broken lives rebuilt, restored, and made useful in passing along the faith to future generations. These families also will add to their own life greater fulfillment.

Our God offers redemption and blessing. Christian stepfamilies have a great opportunity to experience his marvelous grace and pass it along to others. Singing the blues can be therapeutic only briefly. We can emote a little, and maybe have a laugh at our own self-absorbed pathos. But once we've sung our sad song, it's time to refocus on the one who orchestrated the plan and get busy putting his plan into action.

Acknowledgments

Miracle is the only word I can think of to describe the creation of this book. I must first thank the Father for his orchestration of the events in my life over the past several years. He has changed me and, I pray, made me more useful for his purpose, and he has placed people in my life to guide me along the way. This book would not exist if not for those who offered encouragement, expressed enthusiasm, supported me physically and emotionally, and gave their gracious permission for me to use a few of our family stories as examples.

I would like to express my gratitude to my thesis committee at Southwestern Baptist Theological Seminary in Fort Worth, Texas. To Dr. Marcia McQuitty, Dr. Scott Floyd, and Dr. Robert DeVargas, thank you for your sincere enthusiasm, honest feedback, and encouragement to pursue publication of my thesis. Because you believed in this project, my own self-doubts were defeated. A teacher's faith truly makes a difference in a student's life!

Loving thanks to my husband, Carl, who supported me through my seminary career and continues to encourage me in the process of discovering how God wants to use us to help other stepfamilies in their journey. Also, loving thanks to Carl and my stepdaughters, Tracy and Melissa, who permitted me to share some of our family's stories in order to help others.

Thanks also to my mom and dad, Peggy and Fred Simmons, who helped in the editing process early on and continually offered their praise and encouragement. Thanks to many friends and my church family at Bent Tree Bible Fellowship, whose excitement kept me pumped about this project. And thanks to Baker Books and acquisitions editor Vicki Crumpton and associate editor Kelley Meyne (and I'm sure many others before it's all said and done), who took a chance on me!

1

Stepping In

B ooks are often written because someone is experiencing
something for which he or she finds no adequate resources
on the bookshelves. I am a Christian stepmom. During a
difficult time in my relationship with my stepdaughters, I found
very few Christian stepfamily resources to help me. "Why aren't
things working for us? Is it their fault? Is it my fault? Is God working anywhere in our situation? If so, why doesn't he straighten
them out?" These were some of my own questions, and I could
find no satisfactory answers.

Soon I discovered others with common struggles. My church
friends, family members, fellow students on the seminary cam-
pus, a complete stranger with whom I chatted in the waiting
room of a hair salon—many were facing anguishing trials due
to divorce and remarriage. All of us wished we had understood
more about stepfamily life before we entered one.

Our stepfamily relationships changed radically when my youngest stepdaughter came to live with us. Through that experience I
began to suspect that stepfamilies who commit to a Christian way
of life deal with a higher level of conflict.

At least one Christian author shares a similar suspicion. Dr. Archibald D. Hart, a child of divorce and now a psychology professor at Fuller Theological Seminary, says:

> Are the children of Christian parents any better off in a divorce? I believe not. If anything, I would venture to suggest that in many instances they are in a worse situation. Why? In addition to the problems that any child has to face in adjusting to the breakup of the home, the child of Christian parents has to confront the failure of their religious system to resolve the conflict in the home. . . . The child could easily become disillusioned with Christianity and come to seriously question whether spiritual values are helpful or important.[1]

Hart goes on to state that he believes the damaging effects of divorce on children can be minimized. He encourages Christian parents (in spite of their greater challenge) to work toward as healthy as possible a postdivorce life for their children.[2]

The negative effects of divorce on children usually compound when a parent remarries. No matter how a stepfamily came into being—through divorce, widowhood, or marriage of an unwed mother—the soil from which stepfamilies grow, and in which their roots develop, is hard and rocky. Most if not all of the family members deal with ongoing emotional struggles and painful losses.

Therefore, Dr. Hart's encouragement applies to stepparents as well. Stepparents, along with parents, must diligently cultivate that unforgiving soil in order to grow as healthy a stepfamily as possible.

The Step Plight

No family can avoid emotional stresses. However, in a stepfamily, members may feel freer to choose to endure the pain and the strife or run away from it. Lack of blood ties makes a big difference in the level of loyalty and commitment between all

14

stepfamily members. And, as a counselor once told me, the only thing harder than being a parent is being a stepparent.

Over recent years, the number of stepfamilies in America has rapidly increased due to the high number of divorces and remarriages. Statistics reveal the rapid trend away from nuclear families as a norm. For example:

- In 1990, about 20 percent of all children in two-parent households lived with a biological parent and a stepparent.[3]
- In 1992, experts estimated that one in three Americans was a steprelative of some kind, and that half of all Americans would at some point in their lives be connected to a stepfamily.[4]
- Forty-three percent of all marriages in 1997 were remarriages.[5]
- In 1998, 2.2 million marriages took place, compared to 1.1 million divorces that same year.[6]
- About 60 percent of remarriages break up, with blame placed primarily on the presence of children from previous relationships.[7]

In online stepparenting forums, this question sometimes pops up: "If your life as a stepparent is so bad, why do you stay?" Many do not stay, adding further tragedy to the effects of divorce on children. Others stay, only to ignore the highly volatile emotions of children who simmer with an ongoing rage that periodically boils over, many times to burn the stepparents.

In her twenty years of studying children of divorce, Judith Wallerstein found that many kids suffer lifelong anxieties from the divorce.[8] Expecting them to accept stepparents and stepsiblings in their lives may well add to their anxiety.

When compared to children of intact families, children of divorce:

- marry at younger ages and have poorer quality marriages,
- live together more often prior to marriage,

- have lower incomes,
- are more likely to divorce, and
- experience lower levels of well-being in general.

Since their parent role models expose them to unhealthy relationship skills, they do not learn healthy relationship skills, such as building trust, communicating, or managing emotions. Thus, they tend to behave in ways that sabotage relationships, exhibiting harmful traits such as jealousy, control, and manipulation.[9]

These findings should place a huge burden on remarried couples to exemplify loyalty and commitment to marriage and family, no matter the stepfamily turmoil. If the breakup of the first marriage damages a child's chances for lasting relationships, couples must do better the next time around. Paul Amato, a researcher at the University of Nebraska-Lincoln, ended his report *Children of Divorced Parents as Young Adults* by saying, "Given these findings, perhaps the warnings of the conservatives *are* correct. Perhaps we *should* be alarmed about the well-being of the next generation and the future of our society" (emphasis added).[10]

Indeed we should be alarmed. Amato states that with each generation, the negative effects of divorce multiply. He believes the divorce problem can best be addressed by working to increase the number of happy two-parent families.[11] I agree and believe the key to growing more happy two-parent families is in reclaiming the biblical ethic of marriage and family. To do so seems an impossible challenge for our society as a whole. The challenge will be even greater for the growing number of American stepfamilies.

Changing the Step Approach

I often wish I'd had the foresight to research stepfamily life before I entered it. For example, certainly I understood that my husband, Carl, had ongoing financial and relational obligations to his children, and I fully partnered with him in keeping those commitments. However, I didn't consider the unbreakable tie that my husband had with his ex-wife, or how much influence she would have in some decisions he made. Our family climate would always be somewhat controlled by the mother of his children.

Had I researched beforehand, many of the myths I believed and acted on might have been corrected. I might have been better prepared to deal with the explosive emotional hardships of stepfamily life. Therefore, I hope to be of help to other stepfamilies (potential or existing) by addressing the issues I believe to be pivotal for Christian stepfamilies.

Stepping Cleanly through Culture

Cultural trends powerfully impact the opinions and beliefs of everyone within a culture—even Christians. Culture is any element of our existence that we shape with our own actions. Our tangible possessions, our tastes in food, our routines, our values, our traditions, and many other lifestyle choices distinguish one group from another or one person from another. Culture constantly undergoes change, especially in America.

In contrast to culture, God's Word never changes. To determine which cultural changes are beneficial and which are harmful, we must examine any new ideas in light of God's eternal Word. For Christian families, the Bible is a lot like the coffee filter I put in my coffeepot each morning. If I didn't use a filter, I would constantly pick grounds out of my teeth. In the same way, Scripture helps us keep the good about our culture and discard the things that would otherwise spoil the abundant life Christ offers us.

The free will God granted us allows us to use God's creation either to serve and honor him or to serve and honor ourselves. When we focus only on serving ourselves, our culture becomes

17

more fragmented and self-centered—a state of existence that Scripture calls "the kingdom of the world" (Rev. 11:15).

Daily we encounter the kingdom of this world. For example, in recent history we have pondered the ethical dilemmas of embryonic stem cell research, cloning animals and humans, and whether or not to invade a country, among many other issues. Marketing to teens, roller shoes, cell phones for each member of the family, Krispy Kreme donuts—all of these are part of "culture," which impacts my life (and often my waistline!).

Consider this article from the *New York Times* that explains the comfort that the American viewing audience finds in the "spectacularly dysfunctional" Soprano family. Mobster Tony Soprano is described as "a surprisingly good father, at once sternly moralistic and unambivalently loving, and though his marriage is marred by his serial adulteries, he clearly loves Carmela." [12] He is a deeply religious man and believes in God, yet makes his living from violent crime.

Such perversions infect our culture with the idea that it is possible to be at peace with God while committing (or passively allowing) all manner of sinful behavior, including violent crimes against humanity. The Cleavers may have presented an unrealistic, flowers-and-hearts image of family perfection, but the Sopranos present an alternative that defies logic and reason. Yet the writers of Hollywood work it all out in the end, and the seed is planted. We rationalize, "If it can work out for him, certainly my lesser sins will work out for me."

This barrage of new ideas, technologies, and products wearies the discriminating soul to the point that couples and parents stop discriminating, finding it easier to go with the flow. When confronted with godly values that contradict popular ways of thinking, families find it onerous to agree with God, because agreeing with God calls them to engage in battle with the kingdom of this world (and with their own clashing desires). Our culture needs a "values adjustment," and Christian couples need the mind of Christ in the matters of marriage and family.

An Overview

The goals of this book are threefold:

- to help stepfamilies strengthen their marriages and families so that the painful cycle of divorce does not continue,
- to prepare Christian stepfamilies for challenges not typically found in nuclear families, and
- to provide encouragement that no matter what the current circumstances, God can still work his amazing plan in individuals and families.

As I progressed in my own search for answers to my stepfamily dilemmas, God began to teach me about my own faulty belief system that was influenced by both a legalistic religiosity and the culture I live in. Therefore, chapters 2–5 address trendy thinking about family issues and compare that thinking with God's intent found in Scripture, illustrating how far even Christians drift from God's ideal.

Readers anxious to understand stepfamily dilemmas may be tempted to skip over these first chapters. If you do, please return to them. They are like the reset mechanism at the bowling alley that sets downed pins into their correct, upright position. Stepfamily life can skew your view and sometimes knock you right off your feet. So allow your heart to be refreshed with the reality of God's ideal for your marriage and family, and reset that worthwhile family dream.

Chapters 6–12 address some realities of stepfamily life from the point of view of each family member. Chapter 6 discusses why stepfamilies do not work the same as nuclear families. Chapter 7 covers the wounds from the past—the emotional weeds that return to spoil our current situation. Chapters 8–10 offer suggestions for overcoming those weeds through cooperative parenting with former spouses, proactive stepparenting, and constructive discipline. Finally, chapters 11 and 12 discuss how to meet the emotional needs of children of divorce and offer suggestions for improving step relationships (parent to parent, spouse to spouse, adult to child, and kid to kid). Stories depicting stepfamily life, some statistics from stepfamily research, and related insights from Scripture hopefully will help you through difficulties that your stepfamily may encounter. As parents and stepparents begin to understand each other's needs and struggles, as well as those of their children, the greater will be the potential for stepfamily peace and progress.

No matter how well we prepare and work to understand stepfamily dynamics, there will likely be more tension, more challenges, and more relationship struggles than we dream about in our family ideals. For those times when the going gets tough, chapter 13 offers some final thoughts, stories, and encouragements as you work toward God's vision in spite of the rough terrain your stepfamily may travel to reach it. By clinging to his redemptive intentions, you will surely be blessed as God provides meaning and purpose and allows you to become his instrument of healing and grace in your own stepfamily.

2

What Happened to "Happily Ever After"?

When visiting my in-laws, my stepdaughters occasionally moaned about the hardships of being kids. Grandpa's standard consolation: "There, there. It'll all be better when you get married."

Marriage veterans understand the sarcasm in that sentiment and can likely reflect upon a day when they actually believed it to be the truth. Once upon a time, I trusted that marriage would remedy all that ailed me. I can still hear the dreamer of days gone by saying, "I always wanted a big wedding." I can still feel the pain when that dreamer in me confessed, "This is not what I expected."

Perhaps you also have been disillusioned in marriage. Maybe you married into a stepfamily and then had the "this isn't what I thought it would be" epiphany. Nothing is wrong with wanting a nice wedding and a loving marriage and family. But when the happily-ever-after myth collapses, the down-and-dirty reality emerges, at which point husbands and wives may ponder reneging on their promise never to get a divorce.

When the myth collapsed in my first marriage, I began to entertain thoughts of divorce and a more satisfying relationship. I had a choice: "Do I feed the doubts and grow more doubt and dissatisfaction? Or do I deal with the reality of my marriage?" I entertained the doubts, deciding there was no possibility my dream could come true in that set of circumstances. I still blindly believed in "happily ever after."

Then the myth unraveled in my second marriage, and I finally got it. There are no perfect marriages, because there are no perfect people. I needed a new perspective on marriage if this one was going to work. I decided to combat those destructive doubts by letting the light of God's Word help me resolve my marriage philosophy flaws.

Great Expectations

Love, companionship, passion, family—all of these worthy goals for a marriage would make the top-ten list for why people marry. God created in us the longing for these wonderful things. But as with any big dream, the hard part is sitting down and detailing all the costs prior to signing the contract. I laugh at myself when I remember my flippant attitude during premarital counseling:

> Pastor: "What about finances? Who will handle your finances? How will you decide how to spend your money?"
>
> Me: "Well, we think totally alike on that subject. We will balance the checkbook together. We will consult with

each other before making big purchases. That won't be a problem."

Pastor: "What about children? Carl already has children and can't have any more. Don't you want children?"

Me: "Oh, we've talked about that too. We can either adopt, or he said he would have that reversal surgery. That won't be a problem."

Pastor: "Hmmmm."

Me: "Really! It won't be a problem."

And so it went. I wasn't there to receive counsel. I needed to jump through the necessary hoops to get the church's blessing. When couples receive their premarital counseling, it is easy to give all of the right answers to get the "go ahead" from the pastor. But do the idealistic, hopeful couples fully grasp the ramifications of the commitment "for as long as we both shall live"?

Dispelling the Myth about Love

I remember the first time I saw Carl. As I sat in the choir loft during Sunday morning worship, my eyes were drawn like metal shavings to a magnet to a handsome man in a dark suit and his two beautiful little girls. They sat in the left-center section four or five rows from the front. I was not desperate at the time for a man (really!), but I couldn't stop thinking, "What a handsome guy, and what beautiful girls. I wonder where their mother is."

Carl soon joined the singles' group, and we became acquainted. He was a new Christian, and God was leading him to attempt reconciliation with his former wife. His wife came to know the Lord during that season; however, the reconciliation did not work out.

I vividly remember the day he first asked me out. I was working in my cubicle in the general accounting department when the phone rang. Carl had called to invite me to an Amy Grant concert for that very night. As I hung up the phone, I whisper-shouted, "Yes!" Six months later, we married, and never in all that time did I dream about conflict—only harmony and bliss, believing it would last forever.

The bubble didn't take too long to burst. I began to tire of third-floor apartment life and pressured Carl to start house hunting. He struggled with depression, something I didn't know how to handle well. I began to feel as if nothing I did brought him any satisfaction. He tried to make me happy by buying me things that I wanted, or that he thought I wanted. I began to control the finances to make sure we didn't go into debt. The baggage of mistrust that we each carried from prior relationships began to wear us down. We both began to resent the hoops it seemed we had to jump through to "prove" our love.

Many times, human love is all about doing whatever it takes to get the other person to prove his or her love. At its worst, human love is nothing more than a series of manipulations doomed for failure, because control in relationships breeds only resentment.

That *demand* to perform ruins the opportunity for love's free expression. A person can never please his or her partner, because while the right things are now being done, they are done only under coercion. True love, by definition, must be freely offered. If God could have been satisfied with forcing humankind to love him, we would not have been given free will.

Grasping the Truth about "God Love"

The end of that wonderful euphoric state of being in love is not the source of the relationship downfall. God created each part of us—body, mind, and emotions. Therefore, being in love must be another amazing and wonderful intricacy of the human experience designed by God. But God also designed humans so that the euphoria will wane, creating, not a chance for anxiety or abandonment, but an opportunity for love to deepen and grow.

The exciting part about the end of marital bliss is that astonishing chance to move on from the superficial into the divine. In learning to love another person God's way, humanity can begin to understand the extremes of his love for his creation—a love in which God died on the cross to reconcile some truly rebellious creatures to himself.

What is "God love"? It includes elements that rub against the grain of human nature. First Corinthians 13 contains the most complete description of the evidence of this lasting love. These difficult elements reveal the fact that love is not a means to a selfish end, but sacrifices selfish desires for the benefit of the beloved:

> Love never gives up.
> Love cares more for others than for self.
> Love doesn't want what it doesn't have.
> Love doesn't strut,
> Doesn't have a swelled head,
> Doesn't force itself on others,
> Isn't always "me first,"
> Doesn't fly off the handle,
> Doesn't keep score of the sins of others,
> Doesn't revel when others grovel,
> Takes pleasure in the flowering of truth,
> Puts up with anything,
> Trusts God always,
> Always looks for the best,
> Never looks back,
> But keeps going to the end.
> Love never dies. . . .
> Go after a life of love as if your life depended on it—because
> it does.
>
> 1 Corinthians 13:4–8; 14:1 MESSAGE

25

First Corinthians 13 makes love sound like hard work without reward. However, God's thoughts are higher than our thoughts, and his ways higher than our ways. When two people covenant to demonstrate this kind of love to each other and work over the years to perfect their love, they begin to glimpse and experience the perfection of creation before the fall. The joy of a moment of near-perfect love in a marriage makes up for many marital blunders. Over a lifetime, those marital blunders occur less and less often as each partner progresses in his or her ability to love.

Carl and I have been married thirteen years as I write this. Only in the last few years have we emerged from practicing human love for each other into practicing God love. I now understand how important my husband's "cave" is to him and don't pester him to spend all his downtime with me or to keep his space clean. I now trust him with our finances, and the leadership he has demonstrated in our relationship has been wonderful. He solicits my input and considers my feelings in family issues. We still are growing in our ability to love God's way, but even a little change makes a big difference.

Myths and Truths about Companionship

In the same way that human ideas of love bring just the opposite effect, human ideas of companionship can also spoil the marital relationship. Webster's defines *companion* as "one that accompanies another," and as "one employed to live with and serve another." *Companionship* is "the fellowship existing among companions."[1]

In her article "Divorce and the Church," Diana Garland states, "Marriage has been redefined by our culture in the past twenty years. It has become an agreement to live in friendship and support and sexual intimacy with the partner; it is no longer defined as the creation of a new family unit."[2] When I read this, it hit me that *I* had never thought of marriage so profoundly as "the creation of a new family unit." Wow! But how embarrassing that my marriage thinking was still so influenced by the worldly culture I lived in. I thought of my marriage as having someone to live with, someone to be with, someone to do things with. Not as a "unit" in which we focus on fashioning a stable, supportive, life-giving home in order to contribute to the welfare of society as a whole.

The plethora of nightclubs, dating hot lines, singles chat rooms, and recent matchmaking television shows reveals the casual attitudes we have regarding male-female relationships, as well as our lust for new thrills in companionship. I often receive junk e-mails telling me how to increase my abilities to attract the opposite sex or how to have an extramarital affair and keep it a secret. Our culture promotes the attitude of walking away when you become bored with your mate—if we think of each other as friends, then we reserve the freedom to grow apart and move on to a new frontier.

God did create marriage for companionship, but a different sort of companionship. His idea of companionship involves uniting two people who become complete in each other. Genesis 2:19–24 records how God created Eve to be Adam's "suitable helper." A man is to be *united* to his wife, "and they will become *one* flesh" (emphasis added). Part of Webster's last definition of *companion* seems to come closest to God's: living together to serve each other.

God's kind of companionship includes sharing times of leisure, enjoyment, and entertainment together. It includes shared growth but also supporting the other's growth in individual endeavors. It means sticking together in good times and hard times, for physical and emotional strength. It means forgoing individual desires that might harm the family unit, so that family goals can be realized. God's kind of companionship involves sharing a past, a present, and a future.

When Carl and I went through a downtime in our marriage, we each pondered being apart, and we each had an amazing realization: Neither of us could imagine life without the other. The very thought was too painful to bear. This was a true turning point in our marriage. We realized we had become lifelong companions for each other.

Companionship is the aspect of relationship comparable to a system. In a system, each part contributes something necessary to the whole, and the whole is always greater than the sum of its parts. Companionship that works unselfishly for the whole will take on a more profound form than either individual could have dreamed.

Myths and Truths about Passion

Sex is everywhere in our culture; we cannot avoid it. Billboards, magazines, television and film, the Internet, malls, grocery store checkout stands. Sometimes it is as if there could be no life without sex.

In fact, there can be no life without sex. Yes, God created sex too! And everything God creates is good. Until people pervert it.

It should be no great shocker to say that some couples get married primarily for sex—at least those who have some moral scruples and want to make it legitimate. What God intended for intimacy, pleasure, and procreation, humans tend to use selfishly. As with many other parts of God's creation, which become tainted by selfishness, the beauty and goodness of sex becomes perverted into something destructive to people, relationships, and marriages.

Opportunities for us to mess up our sex lives are unlimited. Easy access to pornography causes fantasies of sexual gratification for its own sake. Pornographers depict acts that omit love, respect, and concern for the object of lust, thus removing sex from the realm of love and dumping it into the realm of shame and depravity. The social acceptance of sex outside of marriage causes (1) intimate attachments (especially for women, but also for men) that regularly break, leaving gaping emotional wounds and a heightened inability to trust, and (2) wide-open doors of temptation to cheat on spouses. Having multiple sex partners puts men and women at risk for more than fifty sexually transmitted diseases and can ransack the lives of the innocent children conceived as a result. Amazingly, we are still able to rationalize our injurious behaviors.

God created us with a need for intimacy, and he created sex as the height of many ways to satisfy marital intimacy. Intimacy is a need. Sex is a desire. When someone needing intimacy is preyed upon by someone wanting sex, I believe that is one of the lowest of all human acts. The person desiring gratification becomes his or her own object of love, an act not even remotely representative of God love.

God created everything good. Sex and passion used his way— always to serve and benefit the other within a marriage—become a thing of intimacy, beauty, and mutual gratification, the stuff of Shakespearean sonnets. Keeping passion in the marriage, however, requires the godly traits of perseverance, patience, kindness, cultivation, and open communication.

Have you ever read Song of Solomon aloud with your spouse? Have you ever presented your spouse with a passionate love poem? The lover and the beloved in Song of Solomon had no trouble being clear about their desires (see Song of Sol. 1:2–4, 12–17; 2:3–13; 4:1–7). Yet for some reason, sex is hard for us to talk about. We fear wounding our partner's ego, or maybe our upbringing taught us that talking about sex is shameful. But Genesis 2:25 says, "The *man and his wife* were both naked, *and they felt no shame*" (emphasis added).

Myths and Truths about Family

What is a family? A general definition is "an intimate community of persons bound together by blood, marriage or adoption

29

for the whole of life."[3] This definition could be met in a variety of family orientations, some of which, I'm afraid, offend my conservative sensibilities.

In our world today, gay and lesbian couples want to be made legal. Kids give birth to kids; live-in boyfriends float in and out of the lives of single mothers and their children; mothers have children by multiple fathers; single women use sperm banks to become pregnant without the hassle of a relationship with the father. Then there are foster families, divorced single-parent families, the traditional family made up of a married man and woman and their biological children, families with adopted children, street gangs and mafia that refer to themselves as "family," and of course stepfamilies, the topic of this book.

History of the Family

The "traditional" Western idea of the nuclear family was not always the standard. Pagan Roman families operated as a hierarchy. The father, or *paterfamilias,* was seen as separate from the family but the ruler over it. The whole household, including blood relatives, servants, and other property, belonged to the *familia.* Sex outside of marriage was an accepted social practice. (However, if the wife or daughter of the *paterfamilias* was involved, then sex outside of marriage brought great shame upon a house—quite the double standard.) Divorce and remarriage also found acceptance.[4]

New Testament writings presented household codes that clearly espoused God's ideal of faithfulness to one spouse for life (1 Cor. 7:10–16, 27; Eph. 5:21–6:4; Col. 3:18–21; Heb. 13:4). Nevertheless, it took many years for these ideas to take hold in Christian society. In the early centuries of Christianity, theologians such as Tertullian, Augustine of Hippo, and Jerome in the fifth century began formulating the Christian view of marriage and family. Tertullian narrowed the scope of *familia* to mean primarily blood relatives. Augustine, who struggled against a long-term stronghold of sexual sin, developed a philosophy that shaped marriage tenets for centuries to come. He believed Christian marriage served three basic purposes: procreation, fidelity, and stability.[5]

As the Christian form and traditions of marriage and family solidified, this orientation began to flourish and replace the older conceptions. But recent trends seem to eat away at the biblical family institution.

Is the Christian Family Becoming Extinct?

Many children today do not understand the concept of faithfulness to a relationship. The dreams I remember having as a little girl—for a husband and children until death do us part—cannot be fathomed by some children, because they have never seen or experienced that lifestyle. The definition of family has become very broad.

Family researchers such as Maryann Mason refer to alternate family orientations as "pioneers of sorts."[6] She asserts, "America has evolved away from the norm of the two-parent lifelong married couple in which the husband works in the paid labor force and the wife raises the children, and there is no reason to believe that we are going back."[7]

Indeed, our culture likely will not return to the time when divorce was looked upon as a tragedy, sex before marriage was unacceptable, or same-sex partnerships shocked us. Children that once had a chance to be raised in one stable, clearly delineated setting are confronted with multiple changes in family and relationships in their lives. Based on several generations, we know that the traditional family model works well. We don't know much about these newer family models.

Therefore, the field of family research focuses on trying to diagnose the problems of all family orientations so that families

31

can learn how to make the best of their unique situations. The research itself proves to be beneficial. Without this research, much of this book could not have been written. While these studies should continue, it saddens me that words such as "evolved" and "pioneers" are used in research, implying that newer orientations are in some way improvements on God's design.

The prevalence of divorce, couples living together outside marriage, and the tolerance of alternate lifestyles do seem to threaten the existence of the Christian family. But fear not! Some examples that Scripture gives for families reveal that individual believers in all family orientations (rather than science or politics or "evolution") have control over whether or not the Christian family vanishes from our nation.

Initially God calls for male and female to leave their own parents and cleave to each other as helpmates (Gen. 2:20–24), with the mandate to "be fruitful and increase in number; fill the earth and subdue it" (Gen. 1:28). Following God's order is a healthy beginning to being a Christian family. Yet we often get things out of order. Sometimes we increase in number *before* leaving and cleaving. Sometimes we omit the "cleaving" part altogether, and sometimes we marry but never become equal helpmates for each other.

God's grace, however, keeps the door open to establish the Christian family. Joshua is a good example. He followed God "wholeheartedly" (Josh. 14:8). When Joshua grew old, he petitioned the leaders of the families of Israel to remain faithful to God, first by reminding them of the many difficulties through which God had brought them and then by ending his speech with this challenge:

> Now fear the LORD and serve him with all faithfulness. Throw away the gods your forefathers worshiped beyond the River and in Egypt, and serve the LORD. But if serving the LORD seems undesirable to you, then choose for yourselves this day whom you will serve, whether the gods your forefathers served beyond the

River, or the gods of the Amorites, in whose land you are living.
But as for me and my household, we will serve the LORD.

Joshua 24:14–15

Joshua's challenge foreshadows what it means to be a Christian family: a household yielded to God and set apart for God. Unfortunately, many couples are not united in their commitment to serve the Lord. God graciously understands that dilemma as well, and we see what he has to say about that in Paul's writings. First Corinthians 7:14 states:

> For the unbelieving husband has been sanctified through his wife, and the unbelieving wife has been sanctified through her believing husband. Otherwise [if the believer of the family divorces] your children would be unclean, but as it is, they are holy.

While it is true that every individual must choose or reject Christ for himself or herself, it is also true that whenever a believer who strives to honor God is present in a home, God sees that home as a holy place. The Christian family remains alive.

The Family Dream

Prior to the wedding, couples either individually or together have visions for family. I've always wanted a house in the country, a couple of sons, and horses. I dreamed of a deeply "spiritual" marriage where every day we would pray together and spend time studying Scripture together.

For several years of our marriage, my husband's past prevented him from having many dreams. He could see only as far as the next child-support payment. It frustrated him to hear my visions and dreams, because at that time he could not participate in them.

The individual's family dream cannot become his or her god, however. God alone knows the plans he has for each family

33

and each member in it. Scripture indicates that his dreams for each individual yield prosperity, not harm (Jer. 29:11), and his different dream for each individual works with other dreams to weave together an intricate and beautiful tapestry.

Christian families will dare to make God's eternal dream the goal for which they strive. Couples, whether in first marriages or subsequent marriages, must believe that they themselves, their children, their stepchildren, their grandchildren, and their great-grandchildren can play magnificent roles in that dream, roles that only God knows but that are dependent upon choices made today.

One Final Thought

Throughout Scripture, the stories of husbands and wives and God's dealings with creation are woven together to unveil his plan. The long lineages listed in the Bible are evidence of the fact that God uses families to change the course of history. Since creation, every individual has been part of a well-planned story with the freedom to choose how to affect the outcome.

In the beginning:
Creation of heavens and earth >> Marriage of Adam and Eve >> Children of Adam

X << (You are here!)

In the end:
Children of God >> Marriage of Christ and his church >> Creation of new heaven and earth

Reviewing that story, we can begin to grasp God's amazing, redemptive love and how each of us can intimately experience our awesome Creator. Marriage represents all of the things that God intends for humankind to experience with his Son.

- As a man and his wife become one, so do Christians become one with Christ.
- As man and wife are companions, living together and serving each other, so do Christ and the church live together and serve one another.
- The passion of the marriage relationship mirrors the passion of Christ for us and the passion we should have for him.
- As it takes personal sacrifices to strengthen marriage and family, so did Christ lay down his life for the church, and so must believers make personal sacrifices for the sake of the gospel of Christ.
- As married couples receive extended family, so it is with new believers, who join a worldwide family of spiritual moms and dads, brothers and sisters, and will likely produce spiritual children.

What a tremendous privilege married couples have to point others to the magnificent, redemptive love of God.

Check Your Vision

1. First Corinthians 13 gives us an acid test as to whether we practice human love or God love. Respond to the statements below. Note where the weaknesses are in your own ability to love God's way, then ask him to help you in those areas.

   I give up on others.
   Often   Occasionally   Rarely
   I desire what I don't have.
   Often   Occasionally   Rarely

I keep track of the times others wrong me.

Often   Occasionally   Rarely

I love it when someone grovels to keep me happy.

Often   Occasionally   Rarely

I focus on the weaknesses of others.

Often   Occasionally   Rarely

If I'm not happy, ain't nobody happy.

Often   Occasionally   Rarely

2. Do you primarily perceive your marriage as something that will last as long as you both get your needs met or as an irreversible new entity that can make a difference in the world?
3. What is your dream for your family? How do you believe it compares to God's dream? Your spouse's dream?

3

Breaking the Cycle of Divorce and Remarriage

Barry and Karen, both Christians, had been married for four years. Over the last two years, they'd become increasingly miserable. They each had a child from a previous marriage: Barry had seven-year-old Jason, and Karen had twelve-year-old Beth. Together they had Josh, now in his terrible twos.

Barry and Karen loved their kids, and Barry hoped to be a good father to Beth, whose biological dad had been undependable. But Beth had never become attached to Barry and continued to defend her real father. She also seemed to work hard at driving a wedge between Barry and Karen. Between her discipline problems at school and the lies she told her real father about Barry, Karen and Barry seemed to be constantly putting out a fire somewhere.

Before they married, Barry thought he understood Karen's fears of men—she'd been let down so many times in the past.

But now he realized he could never make up for her past—she wouldn't trust anyone enough to really help her with her insecurities. She always questioned him when he spent time surfing the Internet—afraid he was looking at pornography like her ex did. She called him at work at least three times a day just to be sure he was there. She always looked at him suspiciously when he came home later than usual or when he talked to his ex-wife on the phone. He didn't know how much more he could take.

Surely God has someone who would be better for Karen than me, Barry thought. And if there was a next time for him, he'd be sure that she was emotionally stable—perhaps someone who hadn't been married before.

Karen knew she needed to trust Barry more. He'd never given her a reason not to. But she just couldn't stop the fears. Her ex-husband had lied to her for years, and she wouldn't be played for a fool again. Karen also felt like Barry was too hard on Beth. He just didn't understand all she had been through, and he constantly criticized Beth's behavior and Karen's parenting.

Barry's ex-wife had spent all their money, forcing them into bankruptcy before they divorced. Even though Barry took care of the family well, he watched every penny Karen spent. She felt like a dog on a leash where the finances were concerned. Karen knew her lack of trust was pushing Barry away. But his critical spirit was making it hard for her to trust him. And anger grew inside her over Barry's obsession with money. She wondered how much longer they would be able to hold it together. Maybe she should have just stayed single—life would be so much easier.

"New and Improved" Great Expectations

The above story is fictional but in essence not dissimilar to my own story. Both my husband and I had baggage from past relationships and unrealistic expectations for the future that brought us to a breaking point: Either our marriage would break or our hearts would break for each other. Because we were Christians, neither of us said the *D* word, but both of us secretly hoped the other person would take that leap and shoulder the blame so that we could be free of each other and start over again.

These examples illustrate one way couples who *want* to hold to a strong marriage ethic can begin to consider divorce. Once the marriage ends, they emerge with long mental lists, new dreams, each item of which begins with "Next time . . ." They believe they now have a clear understanding of what type of person (if any) will make them happy and how to prevent future relationship problems. Some make up rules for future relationships, which they hope will protect them from a repeat ending. The rules easily get broken, because the desire to once again experience love, passion, and closeness is more than wounded people can bear. They also make sincere promises, saying, "Next time, divorce will not be an option."

Unrealistic expectations brought into marriage, plus the ease of obtaining a legal divorce, equals a skyrocketing number of broken homes. Were it not for God's grace that barely held Carl and me accountable to him, we would once again be among the one in four American adults to opt for divorce.[1]

According to Barna Research, born-again Christians *beat* the one-in-four national average with one in three adult believers having been through divorce.[2] Seventy-five percent of these will remarry, and about 60 percent of these remarriages will also end in divorce.[3] And the cycle of divorce and remarriage goes on as we somehow fail to recognize all the ramifications of reneging on our marital covenant.

Wallerstein's studies indicate that many marriages that dissolve can be described as "moderately unhappy" rather than extreme incompatibilities or cases of abuse or unfaithfulness.[4] What we term "irreconcilable differences" often could be reconciled.

39

Members of the American Academy of Matrimonial Lawyers wrote a booklet called *Making Marriage Last.* They had this to say on the topic of why marriages fail:

> Not all marriages fail for the same reason. Nor is there usually one reason for the breakdown of a particular marriage. Nevertheless, we hear some reasons more often than others. They are: poor communication, financial problems, a lack of commitment to the marriage, a dramatic change in priorities, and infidelity. There are other causes we see a lot, but not quite as often. They are: failed expectations or unmet needs; addictions and substance abuse; physical, sexual or emotional abuse; and lack of conflict resolution skills.[5]

Another article states that the Internet is now being blamed as a cause of marital strife. The *BBC News* article notes that time spent on the Internet takes time away from spouses, and the possibility of online infidelity and pornography poses a serious threat to marriages.[6]

Many of these causes for divorce can be turned around if both parties recognize the priority that should be given to marriage and family and take healthy steps to resolve them.

Truths about Divorce and Remarriage

When people have strong desires for something they know to be either wrong or questionable, they often polarize themselves toward the arguments *for* their desires and *away* from those that remind them of their responsibility or of what is moral and right.

Christians with their minds geared for a divorce likely will search the Scripture for some nugget of truth to justify their actions in pursuing divorce. Many may legitimately find biblical justification, such as cases of adultery. Many will not. Others may not seek wisdom in Scripture at all. Those who don't might also avoid church and other Christians for as long as it takes to complete the marriage breakup. What are some of those truths of divorce and remarriage that are so hard to seek out in times of deep marital conflict?

My pastor often says, "A text without a context is a pretext for a proof-text," which basically means, "Don't use Scripture sound bites for motive validation." If, in all honesty, couples look to God's Word for guidance (rather than for justification of a desired action), they must consider the whole of Scripture. While the New Testament does not give black-and-white answers to the questions of divorce and remarriage, some things are clear.

Truth #1: Divorce does not mean the marriage never happened.

Anyone who divorces his wife and marries another woman commits adultery against her. And if she divorces her husband and marries another man, she commits adultery.

                                                             Mark 10:11–12

Jesus taught his disciples that remarriage entails adultery. In Matthew 5:32 Jesus said that when a man divorces his wife, assuming she has not already been unfaithful, the divorcing husband effectively *causes* both her and her next husband to commit adultery. A close look at these and other divorce passages reveals three important insights as to the ramifications of divorce.

First, by noting that subsequent marriages result in adultery, Jesus points out the permanence of some aspects of the marriage bond. Jesus expresses that reality in another way in Mark 10:8–9: "And the two will become one flesh. So they are no longer two, but one. Therefore what God has joined together, let man not separate." Even though divorce ceases marital obligations to each other, they were once two who became one, and the one has been ripped apart.

My actions to dissolve the contract between my first husband and myself stopped our journey together and sent us on diverging paths. But our time together changed me. The experiences we had together, for better or worse, are in my memory and will affect the way I think and act and love today and until I die. Had my current husband and I dissolved our contract, the same would be true. With each passing relationship, we stuff more worms in our can, so to speak.

Second, both Jesus and Paul acknowledge the likelihood of remarriage, in spite of the fact that it will cause adultery. Jesus assumes in both Matthew 5 and Mark 10 that a divorced person will remarry. Paul states with regard to "the unmarried and the widows" that it is good to stay unmarried but better to be married than to burn with passion (1 Cor. 7:8–9). Later he states that if an unbelieving spouse abandons the believing spouse, the believer is no longer bound to the unbeliever; peace is the greater good (1 Cor. 7:15).

I do not believe that remarriage is the evil being condemned. Rather, it seems that Jesus wants to be clear that while divorce can protect former spouses from each other, consequences and complications beyond our understanding are unavoidable and become greater as future relationships emerge.

Third, when Jesus speaks about divorce, he recognizes that there are perpetrators and there are victims.

- The wife who divorces her husband and remarries sins against her first husband (Mark 10:12).
- The husband who divorces and remarries sins against his first wife (Mark 10:11).
- The husband who divorces his faithful wife *causes* her and her new husband to commit adultery (Matt. 5:32).

A relevant statement made by Jesus is found in Luke 17:1–3 (emphasis added):

Jesus said to his disciples, "Things that *cause* people to sin are bound to come, but woe to that person through whom they come. It would be better for him to be thrown into the sea with a millstone tied around his neck than for him to *cause* one of these little ones to sin. So watch yourselves."

Isn't it a fresh wind of grace to hear Jesus acknowledge that "stuff happens"? Sometimes we are led into sin by things and people beyond our control. Perpetrators and victims both exist in the divorce scenario. Parties to a divorce may be either the perpetrator or the victim, or they could both be perpetrators and victims of each other's hurtful actions. The perpetrator(s), it appears, will be held highly accountable. Sometimes we dishonestly seek to be sinned against in order to appear the victim. In that case, who truly is the perpetrator? (So watch yourselves!)

The children will always be victims. In society's understanding of divorce, the impossibility of complete divorce is initially hard to accept. However, it soon becomes apparent when children and stepchildren are part of the picture.

Truth #2: Divorce results from multiple sins that harden hearts— either the husband's heart against the wife, the wife's against the husband, or both hearts against each other.

Jesus replied, "Moses permitted you to divorce your wives because your hearts were hard. But it was not this way from the beginning."

Matthew 19:8

The term *divorce* refers to the public, legal ending of a marriage contract. But a private, emotional divorce typically takes place long before the public one. "A couple may live under the same roof with a legal marriage contract, but because of the poisonous anger and alienation that pervade their relationship, they are no less guilty of breaking their vows to love and cherish one another until death."[7]

The serious hurts husbands and wives inflict on each other while on the path to legal divorce must grieve God terribly. At

43

least one of the spouses in the relationship maintains a firm policy of sinning against the other, and eventually those marriage values—things like compassion, love, and self-sacrifice—become so badly seared that only numbness and anger remain in one spouse, if not both.

Jesus makes it clear that divorce was created neither for the purpose of making the marriage as if it never happened nor for the purpose of setting the partners free for another relationship. God allowed divorce for one basic reason: to break a cycle of stubborn cruelty that one or both spouses inflict on a marriage.

Scripture tells how to prevent those sinful behaviors in marriage that lead to a hard heart. In Ephesians 5:21–32 Paul describes appropriate heart attitudes a husband and wife should demonstrate to each other: submission, love, respect, and sacrifice with a desire to build the other person up into a "radiant" being without stain, wrinkle, or blemish. Then in Galatians 5:19–21 Paul warns against the works of sinful nature that serve to destroy people, especially in the context of marriage:

> The acts of the sinful nature are obvious: sexual immorality, impurity and debauchery; idolatry and witchcraft; hatred, discord, jealousy, fits of rage, selfish ambition, dissensions, factions and envy; drunkenness, orgies, and the like.

Without confession of the sins spouses commit against each other, without repentance, forgiveness, and commitment to stop the hurtful behaviors, the only possible ending to a marriage is alienation, animosity, and emotional divorce.

Truth #3: God has the power to "un-harden" hearts.

> I will give them an undivided heart and put a new spirit in them; I will remove from them their heart of stone and give them a heart of flesh. Then they will follow my decrees and be careful to keep my laws. They will be my people, and I will be their God.
>
> Ezekiel 11:19–20

The most important truth many Christian couples choose not to factor into their situation is their direct connection to the one who has the power to bring healing and reconciliation in any situation. When Jesus taught about divorce in Matthew 19, he did so in response to pointed questions from the religious rulers who wanted to test him. Their question: "Is it lawful for a man to divorce his wife for *any* and every reason?" (Matt. 19:3, emphasis added). We still ask that question today, as lobby groups fight for divorce reform.

Much controversy existed because of the two diverse viewpoints taught by the most prominent rabbis of the time. Jesus answered the religious leaders but neither confirmed nor denied the legality of a man divorcing his wife for *any* reason. What he did do was focus on God's ideal for marriage from the beginning, the fact that man and wife become one. The kingdom of God inside the believer enables the heart of stone to be replaced with a heart of flesh, which makes it possible for believers to fulfill that higher moral standard in which divorce is unnecessary.[8]

I'm Divorced and Remarried— What Now?

Believers who not only want their stepfamilies to make it, but also want to provide a home where each person has the best chance to grow and be loved, need only to work toward remaining faithful to God's call and obedient to his Word.

First of all, understand that Jesus died for *all* sin. Repentance and forgiveness are keys to healing in a believer's life. Maybe you were the victim. You sincerely did all you knew to do to prevent a broken marriage, but to no avail. You likely have many hurts that need to be healed. Seeking God's comfort, peace, healing, and protection can be your first step. Then allowing him to guide you through a process of forgiveness for wrongs done to you will help you move on to a new life of increased understanding, less encumbered by your past, with an empathy for others in similar situations.

In my case, I was a perpetrator. It took me about five years after my divorce to admit that. During that time, something kept me from becoming the spiritual person I really wanted to be. When I was among those I admired at my church for their close walk with Christ, I felt as if I were always on the outside looking in. Then one day, by God's grace, I fully realized and accepted the magnitude of my action. I had hurt my first husband and his family. I had also presumed upon God's grace, expecting his instant forgiveness without my true repentance. The day I really repented and in obedience to God sought forgiveness from my former husband I began a real spiritual journey that I have never regretted.

An honest heart examination with prayerful obedience to God's instructions will begin the healing process. If, like me, you presumed upon God's grace in order to obtain that divorce, you must repent of that presumption, as well as for any other personal responsibility in the marriage breakup, to unlock the chains of the past. First John 1:9 promises that God is faithful to forgive and cleanse all sin confessed to him.

Second, allow the Holy Spirit to teach you how to be the husband or wife your current partner needs, the parent your children need, and the role model your stepchildren need. The first section of this book presents the ideal for which Christians should strive in any family situation, and in which they will find true purpose and fulfillment in their families—even in the second family and with stepchildren. Reading this section in an attitude of prayerful reflection will start the process of submitting to the Holy Spirit and gaining God's perspective.

Third, examine attitudes toward current family relationships, whatever the circumstance may be, and allow them to be scrutinized by God's Word. Is your spouse's former spouse causing you to feel insecure or inferior? Are your stepkids driving you crazy? Do you maintain an emotional attachment to a former spouse that, deep down, you know should be severed? Do you feel sabotaged by your stepkids or your spouse in the area of child discipline? Are your own children guilting you into parenting decisions you know are not truly in their best interest? Are you wondering if stepfamily life is for you?

Wherever you have a grating irritation between your mind and heart, commit to resolve it in such a way that God can work his perfect plan in your life. Don't polarize yourself to the side where you have the illusion of an "easy" out. Don't fear seeking qualified help from other believers. Many people have taken this stepfamily journey and can offer support, accountability, and guidance.

Fourth, understand (really understand!) that while forgiveness for divorced and remarried people is no less possible than forgiveness for stealing a pencil from an employer, forgiveness does not make a divorce "over." Former spouses are intricate parts of each others' lives, and future relationships will be affected. The presence of children creates one unbreakable yet very fragile bond with the former spouse in rearing the children produced together. This takes us to our next topic of exploration: parenting.

Check Your Vision

1. List some of your past or present mind-heart struggles (where your heart wanted something that your values and beliefs fought against).
2. If the struggle was in your past, how was it resolved? If in the present, how do you intend to resolve it? On which side of the struggle do you believe God stands?
3. How is your heart toward members of your stepfamily? Is it hard, or has God already given you "a heart of flesh" toward them? Pray and ask God to give you his vision for your marriage, your children, and your stepchildren.

47

4

The High Call
of Parenting

Remember P. D. Eastman's children's book *Are You My Mother?* The little robin hatches out of his egg while his absent mother looks for food to feed him. Wanting desperately to be with his mother, he hazards a long fall out of his nest in order to find her. Since he's never seen his mother, he mistakes a variety of animals and vehicles for her, experiencing many disappointments and scary moments until he and his mother are finally united.

The story of the little robin reminds me of some sad humor in an episode of *The Simpsons*, when the second-grade teacher, Mrs. Krabappel, passes out cartons of milk to Bart's class for a snack. Whiny, clueless Ralph absentmindedly asks the teacher, "Mommy, can you open my milk?" Over a chorus of snickering classmates, Mrs. Krabappel flatly replies, "I'm not your mother, Ralph."

I also am reminded of a real-life, heartbreaking phone call to Dr. Laura Schlessinger's radio program. A fifteen-year-old girl called to ask if she would be morally wrong if she didn't oblige her father's request for a blood sample. He wanted to have his paternity tested. He no longer wanted to be her father.

Thus, the little bird's story is comforting compared to the realities some children face these days. Many dads and moms in American culture are truly absent from their children's lives, so much so that churches, public education, and social programs pick up more and more of the slack every year. But parents who hope to stem the tide of irresponsible parenting need to be grounded in the attitudes and actions that make for good parenting and wary of those that don't.

While later chapters deal with some specific how-tos, this chapter will discuss these parenting foundations: What is a good parent? What ideologies creep in to lessen a parent's influence over his or her children? What does the Bible say to parents?

What Is a Parent?

The word *parent* is packed with meaning. Webster's first definition is fairly broad: "one that begets or brings forth offspring." Many people fall into this classification of parent. The second definition reaches the heart of what it means to be a parent and includes those who did not beget the offspring (i.e., stepparents, among others): "a person who brings up and cares for another."[1]

The phrase "brings up" is also packed with meaning. It implies hands-on, long-term involvement. For mothers, it begins with prenatal care, when parent and child are physically bonded together. That bond becomes emotional rather than physical as soon as the child exits the womb and the cord is cut. For all kinds of parents, whether biological, adoptive, foster, or "step," bringing up a child means spending the child's formative years in relational involvement, protection, and provision, providing guidance and encouragement with the goal of releasing a competent citizen who will contribute to his or her world.

Ongoing Relational Involvement

Feeding, dressing, bathing, playing, changing, cuddling, watching for signs of distress or illness, providing stimulation for proper development of the senses—all of these require a parent's continuous physical and emotional involvement to instill in infants a sense of security and of belonging. Those early years are crucial, as children have no choice but to be wholly dependent on their parents to meet every single need.

What parent can forget a child's first word, first steps, first time to use the potty chair, or first time to ride a bicycle? Recalling how that little child beamed as parents clapped their hands and cheered "Yea!" should be a poignant reminder of how a parent's ongoing presence ignites children with the fire to keep going and to feel safe to succeed or even make failed attempts at new skills.

The way a parent goes about meeting a child's developmental needs will be that child's training ground for future relationships. Parents can either strengthen or weaken connections through verbal communication, touch, and facial expression, and through listening—or not listening—to their children. The kinds of connections parents develop with their kids will set the precedent for the children's relationships with others throughout life.

Ongoing relational involvement is quite a challenge for stepfamilies. When a stepparent moves in, suddenly a parent's attentions become less focused on relating to the kids and more focused on the new spouse. The kids might not want a new parent in the home and may resist establishing a relationship with the stepparent.

The nonresidential kids, while usually welcomed in the home on the surface, can still sense any negative nonverbal messages from their new stepparent: "I love you, but . . ." Then, after everyone spends the visitation time adjusting, they return to their separate homes.

For many stepfamilies, ongoing relational involvement is not possible in the traditional sense. Extra effort must be put forth by stepcouples to complete this task well.

Protection and Provision

Parents are solely responsible for the health and safety of their children. This is a fundamental parenting concept. Yet our newspapers carry frequent stories of gross parental negligence and horrible abuses that many children suffer at the hands of their parents. Can parents really claim to understand that they are responsible for raising morally upright children when they expose them to pornography on television, in movies, and on the Internet? When they buy them violent Nintendo games and desensitize them to the seriousness of playing with real guns? When the children must come home from school to an empty house and microwave their own junk food?

Parents are solely responsible for the health and safety—physical, mental, emotional, and spiritual—of their children. Once again, this task can be more problematic in stepfamilies than in intact homes. The broken relationship between biological parents often exposes children to many hostile emotions between the two people they need most in the world.

Guilt may cause biological parents to relax their parenting styles to compensate for the broken home. This response can be disastrous for a child's development as he or she learns to use guilt to manipulate parents and others. In the teen years, parents will likely regret the loss of authority they need to protect teens from risky behaviors. When a stepparent tries to correct the parent's lenient style, he or she becomes the "bad guy" in the eyes of the stepchild.

A stepcouple may work hard to protect children and stepchildren from harmful influences, but they cannot control what happens in the other home. Provision also becomes a sensitive issue. Those who pay child support begin to resent lack of control over how their funds are used. The tasks of protection and provision can be done well in stepfamilies when the child's long-term best interests are always a priority, but stepcouples must live with the fact that some things are beyond their control in that realm.

Guidance and Encouragement

Parents provide important and powerful feedback to children as they test their world. This feedback may come in many forms: instruction, praise, correction, discipline, leading, or cheering on, among others.

Praise for right behaviors and personal achievement is perhaps the most necessary element, and often the hardest to give. The first step in earning praise is the responsibility of the trainer: to provide thorough instruction and guided practice on the task to be learned. Often we cannot find something praiseworthy in our children because we haven't done our part—we expect them to inherently know how to accomplish the task. We set our children up for our criticism.

Even when good instruction is provided, all children stray from the acceptable path from time to time and need a course adjustment. Concerned parents will take the time to correct attitudes or behaviors that are unacceptable for reaching the desired destination. Concerned parents will not be afraid to be the authority figures in the lives of their children.

One of the best examples I have seen of parents who guide and encourage their children is my brother and his wife. They are teaching their children to regulate their own behavior, whether parents are nearby or not. From time to time, my nephew comes to my house for an overnight stay. I remember one visit when he was about eight and he had been playing in another room as my husband and I watched the movie *Father of the Bride* on television. Having been trained well to "be careful little eyes what you see," he entered the family room where we sat, on his way to the kitchen, and very carefully avoided even glancing at the television until he confirmed with us that it was okay for him. He even asked if the characters played by Steve Martin and Diane Keaton were legally married!

In another incident, my seven-year-old niece traveled with my mom and dad and me on a trip to Colorado. She had sampled my mom's chocolate chip cookies and also ate one of my peanut butter cookies. Then Meemaw suggested that we drive through the Dairy Queen for a Blizzard.

At first her eyes lit up, but when asked what she wanted in the drive-through lane, those bright baby-blues began to well up with crocodile tears as she said, "I don't care for anything, thank you." She turned her head away from us as the three of us tried to talk her into getting something, or at least sharing something with us. Again her little voice quivered, "I don't care for anything, thank you." Our hearts were broken! What had we done to crush this precious child?

In a few minutes, she regained her composure and cheerfully confessed, "I really did want something, but Mommy said I should try to have only one sweet a day." We were speechless and humbled and awed by her discipline—something each of us lacked sorely in our own diets. We apologized for tempting her and promised to help her in her goal for the rest of the trip. She never had more than one sweet per day and some days turned down a lesser sweet in order to get something she really wanted later on.

My brother and his wife are quite unified and intentional in the things they teach their children. Stepcouples can be unified as well, but becoming unified requires addressing the many additional emotional strains inherent to stepfamily life. For example, nonresidential parents naturally desire to build good memories with their children during visitations and are often reluctant to spend time in a "guidance" mode. Stepparents get caught in the comparison trap, comparing biological children to their stepchildren, and often become more critical than encouraging.

A child without strong adult guidance or encouragement is a child without direction, without skills to find his or her way, and without a sense of purpose or belonging. By default, his or her only guidance comes from peer groups and advertisers who promote self-gratification. Thus, the get-it-while-you-can-anyway-you-can mentality that some teens follow today.

The Goal: Competence

The ultimate goal of all parental effort is to bring up a child who perseveres through life, enjoys life and people, and makes a positive difference somehow, somewhere. Competence (the sense of self-sufficiency plus the skills that contribute) helps a child belong. The first opportunity for belonging is found in the family where a child seeks to be accepted as an integral part.

I can point to several things that my parents did to help me feel competent and a part of our family. First, I was the one who did the dusting and the vacuuming. (My mother trained me well in the right ways to dust and vacuum!) My parents sent me to Sunday school every week with an offering, teaching me the priority of giving to make a difference. My father taught me that I was not the athletically impaired child I thought I was when he spent time teaching me how to play tennis. I learned to be a part of life in my family, rather than fearing that I did not matter at all.

The stresses of stepfamily life can keep us in a "let's just get through this week" mentality, rather than proactively implementing strategies to help a child feel a sense of belonging and contribution to the family. Stepfamilies focus on avoiding tension rather than instilling competence. Failure to instill competence when children are young will make those already difficult adolescent years an even greater challenge.

Relating, protecting, providing, guiding, and encouraging— these are the basic tasks of a parent. That list of responsibilities really doesn't sound ominous. Yet when we find that it requires letting go of some of the freedoms and pleasures of which we are so fond, and that the challenges are greater in stepfamilies, that dissonant recording cranks up again: "Of course I love my children and stepchildren. But what about *me?*"

The Lures of Popular Parenting

Most parents (and stepparents) deeply crave the opportunity and experience of investing their own life in bringing up a child. But American culture and its plethora of possibilities create many competing loyalties in our lives. They bait us away from what is real to what is an illusion.

Lure #1: "What about me?"

As discussed in chapter 2, marriage is perceived by many in our culture to be a 24/7 friend-and-lover relationship focused on personal fulfillment, rather than the creation of a new, permanent entity called "family." When children enter the picture, adults are forced to make choices between personal desires and parental responsibilities. They often try to have both, but the child gets the short end of the stick.

Some rituals in this "me" religion include making careers and personal lives a priority over children, such physically destructive acts as alcohol and drug abuse, and other more passive acts like spending most of our "family time" zoned out in front of our televisions. We sometimes perceive parenting duties as an unfulfilling burden, rather than the rewarding and creative building project they can be. As we reclaim a biblical perspective on our families, we will begin to understand that true fulfillment is attained when we realize "it isn't all about *me*!"

Lure #2: "All my friends do it."

When we had to say no to my stepdaughter, most of the time I knew we made the right decision. But if my husband and I were making right decisions regarding her, why did guilt, doubts, and remorse rise up against our peace of mind? The emotions that overcame us were dizzying and draining. Then the few times we gave in to something against our better judgment, why did we feel so much better?

We as parents don't want to feel bad, so we avoid doing things to make our kids feel bad. We fear being wrong, or scorned by our kids or their friends, or criticized by their friends' parents or their teachers or anybody else. We want to look good, and if we look good compared to others, we'll feel good.

Lure #3: "My kids deserve a better life."

Unresolved bitterness from childhood sometimes pressures parents to supply for their own kids what they wished they could have had. They may also hope to avoid things that they hated about their own childhood.

To a degree, these motivations can be productive in rearing a child. Certainly a parent who grew up in an alcoholic home should be praised for making sure that his or her child does not grow up in that same environment. However, if by "better life" parents mean more *material* wants (not needs), the pleasure in providing for the kids will feed that greed monster working to claim their hearts. Children then cannot learn that they have the ability to be content or provide for themselves. Such indulgence robs children of their own self-discovery.

Lure #4: "Self-esteem! Self-esteem! Self-esteem!"

Those who stress the importance of self-esteem are rightly concerned with stopping the destructive ways that some parents communicate with their children. Calling children "stupid" or "idiot," telling them they will never amount to anything, criticizing and belittling their honest attempts to achieve a goal—such negativity imprisons children in cages of insecurity and fear of trying, thus causing them to fulfill the negative prophecies of their parents.

Ironically, the self-esteem outcry imprisons many parents in cages of insecurity and fear. Our fears of damaging self-esteem freeze us in our parenting to the point that we provide little guidance or discipline. Somehow we've come to believe that we must turn a blind eye to lack of effort. Somehow we have come to believe that sharing truth with our children about their self-destructive behaviors damages them. This is the ultimate illusion!

Lure #5: "I can't control my kid. So why try?"

My husband and I have heard this argument more than once: "You can't control them forever." Obviously that is a true statement, but whenever I hear someone argue this point, I thankfully remember other parents who have set examples for us and supported us in setting and maintaining boundaries. I also thankfully remember my own parents, who even when I was in my midtwenties warned me when they saw me walking toward a dangerous cliff. I didn't like it at the time, but their concern still served as a safety rail, keeping me from stepping off too far.

Kids want and need boundaries, which help them develop a conscience. I remember my stepdaughter telling us that she hears our voices in her head when she's driving her car. "Slow down!"

"Stop following so close!" "Look before you change lanes." She said it was like "that whole conscience thing."

No standards means no conscience. Some kids learned this the hard way and in spite of their parents. The following rules for parents were written by some rehabilitated teens and published on a troubled teens web site:

- Make the rules clearer.
- Parents, present a unified front.
- Don't allow us to control the boundary line; we will keep changing it.
- Don't give up on discipline.
- Make reasonable consequences, ones YOU can keep, then hold to them no matter what!
- Don't discuss rules with us or ask us if we agree with them or like them—we don't, but we need them.
- Don't be afraid to invade our privacy. If we're in trouble, you should read our letters, check our closets, check our friends.
- Don't let us wear you down.
- Don't blame others for our problems.
- Don't be intimidated by us, don't back off, and don't walk on eggshells with us.
- You're not obligated to supply us with money to go out, especially when we've been acting out.
- Demand phone numbers and call to check to see if we are there.[2]

Let the voices of these teens who have been through it overpower any voices shouting, "You can't make a difference." Parents who don't attempt authoritative control will make a difference, but for the worse.

Greater Good Parenting: Obeying That Still, Small Voice

"Your kids need you." The noble call is not a glamorous one. It involves loss of sleep for the next eighteen years (some years more than others); being the adult provider/protector rather than the dependent, self-absorbed child; becoming a boss, a teacher, a counselor, a coach, a private detective, a doctor, a disciplinarian, a banker, a giver of unconditional love that may or may not be reciprocated, and a companion; and knowing when to put on which hat. These tasks can be done not from a self-serving drive, and not to serve the child, but to serve the well-being of the family and each individual in it, and ultimately to serve God and make a difference in the world.

The Greater Good of the Person

> Listen, my son, to your father's instruction
> and do not forsake your mother's teaching.
> They will be a garland to grace your head
> and a chain to adorn your neck.
>
> Proverbs 1:8–9

The Book of Proverbs is a parent's greatest manual for what to teach children "for their own good." Lesson number one: the fear of the Lord.

According to Proverbs, all true knowledge begins with a healthy fear and respect for God and his divine right to reign in our lives (Prov. 1:7). Those who reject this reality effectively accept the identity of a "fool" who despises wisdom and discipline. Those who choose not to fear the Lord actually hate knowledge, and the evil they produce will be perpetrated back upon them (Prov. 1:29–32).

60

A life that fears God demonstrates trusting God above your own reason (3:5–6), honoring God with your wealth (3:9), sleeping restfully (3:24), doing good to others when able (3:27), avoiding the ways of evil men (4:14), guarding the heart against evil and perverse things (4:23), and many other behaviors that defy our natural inclinations. Children must be taught what it means to fear God. If this lesson is taught well by parents who strive to live it themselves, then all subsequent lessons for living a productive life are undergirded by the most worthy of all reasons—pleasing God.

Children who develop an enduring reverence for God and know the precepts of right living are more likely to experience integrity, stability, and confidence in their personhood, and the Hebrew concept of peace, or *shalom,* a sense of wholeness and well-being. The lessons of Proverbs are vitally important to children, for "it is [their] life" (4:13).

One other lesson must also be taught for the good of the person. While this lesson is not in Proverbs, it is the key for living the life described in Proverbs. That lesson would be the salvation message. No greater story can be imparted to a child than that of Christ's love for him or her.

An early understanding that many things we do displease God, that we can't do enough good things to make up for our wrong behaviors, and that Jesus took our punishment for us—these concepts prepare children to place their trust in Christ alone for forgiveness of sin and receive the gift of life forever with him in heaven. One study reported that 86 percent of all believers make their decisions for Christ by age fourteen.[3] The gospel message is the most important instruction a parent can impart to his or her child, for it is eternal life.

The Greater Good of the Family

Scripture has little to say specifically to the inner workings of the family unit. Ephesians 6:1–4 and Colossians 3:18–21 each command children to honor and obey their parents, "for this is right," with the promise "that it may go well with you." In the same passages, Paul commands fathers not to exasperate or embitter their children, but to train and instruct them in the ways of God.

In 1 Thessalonians 2 Paul describes the activity of a mother who gently cares for her children (v. 7) and the role of a father who encourages, comforts, and urges his children to live good lives (v. 12). In 1 Timothy a man who desires to have responsibility in the church must already have obedient children who give him proper respect, and he must manage his household well. The instructions are brief, but they have weighty results.

What habits form from learning to obey and honor parents? First, children learn to respect others and to place responsibility for others ahead of their own needs. Becoming an obedient child means becoming a responsive child. To respond, a child must first have listened to the person giving the command and must have clearly received the message. A child must also recognize the authority of the person giving the command.

So obedience involves listening, understanding, responding, and submitting to an authority figure. These things do not happen naturally; even parents with the highest standards struggle daily to maintain them. When parents engage in the struggle to faithfully teach obedience, they teach many other character traits that result in the well-being of the family.

The Greater Good of the World

Everything learned through family interaction has greater implications for good or for evil in the community, for future generations, and therefore perhaps even the world. Sharing and generosity are virtues that do not naturally develop. Children must be taught how to give to one another and to those in need. The family is the first place we can learn to respect the property of others, to watch out for the welfare of others, and to be a contributor to a solution rather than a part of the problem. Families who promote relationships over material things teach children, as someone has aptly put it, "to love people and use things, rather than to use people and love things." Benevolence begins in the home but does not stop there.

An article in *Better Homes and Gardens* tells the story of a mother who decided to take family benevolence outside the home. She volunteered herself and her three young children to visit and entertain at a senior adult day care center. She knew the volunteer efforts were impacting her children's outlook when her eight-year-old son asked to read for the younger neighborhood children and her twelve-year-old daughter turned down a day at an amusement park to spend time at the senior center. From such experiences, children learn how to be kind and to correct the stereotypes of those they perceive to be different. Children whose parents volunteer are twice as likely themselves to become volunteers in adulthood.[4]

Cooperation, conflict resolution, and negotiation abilities also begin in the home. Parents who work diligently on these skills with their kids teach them how to work productively with others with whom they may not always agree. They also learn how to maintain the integrity of their convictions when they are challenged. These character traits and many others can and should be developed in the home to raise new generations that honor the fast of the Lord as quoted in Isaiah 58:6–8:

> Is not this the kind of fasting I have chosen:
> to loose the chains of injustice
>   and untie the cords of the yoke,
> to set the oppressed free
>   and break every yoke?
> Is it not to share your food with the hungry
>   and to provide the wanderer with shelter—
> when you see the naked, to clothe him,
>   and not to turn away from your own flesh and blood?

Then your light will break forth like the dawn,
    and your healing will quickly appear;
then your righteousness will go before you,
    and the glory of the LORD will be your rear guard.

To the Honor and Glory of God, and for His Kingdom

I believe God created the family to teach many things. First, when children defy their parents' instructions given for their well-being, parents sense a little of the agony God feels when they defy him. Second, families teach lessons about real love: not a feeling, but faithfulness to others in spite of feelings. Third, families are the training camp of human relationships where we learn patience, perseverance, and forgiveness.

Such godly character traits exhibited to the world point others to the one for whom they are labeled. And that is the whole point.

As parents train their children to fear the Lord, to respect and care for others, and to make a difference in the world, and as they provide their children with the knowledge of Christ and opportunities to lay personal claim to Christian faith, parents will fulfill the words of Christ in Matthew 5:14–16:

> You are the light of the world. A city on a hill cannot be hidden. Neither do people light a lamp and put it under a bowl. Instead they put it on its stand, and it gives light to everyone in the house. In the same way, let your light shine before men, that they may see your good deeds and praise your Father in heaven.

Then perhaps one day if you ask your grown children who you were for them in their life, they will tell you:

        You were not my peer.
        You were not a television.

You were not my slave.
You were not a pushover.
You were not my bankroll.
You were not self-serving, or evil, or uncaring.
You were my guide,
and you were my parent.

Check Your Vision

On a scale of 1–5 (1 = ineffective and 5 = very effective), rate yourself in the following areas of parenting and stepparenting:

1. Interacting with my child in a positive manner. _____
2. Thoroughly instructing my child in new endeavors.____
3. Praising progress made even if total success was not achieved. _____
4. Protecting my child from negative influences. _____
5. Providing correction when my child strays. _____
6. Providing meaningful "family times." _____
7. Backing up my words with actions. _____
8. Not falling for the lures of popular parenting (i.e., "What about me?" "All my friends do it!" "Times have changed!" "Your kids deserve a better life," "Self-esteem!" "You can't control them forever!"). _____
9. Teaching and instilling godly values. _____
10. Living out the godly values I teach. _____

5

God Uses Imperfect Families

A normal tendency in stepfamilies is to despair over what seems to be a losing battle: never being able to achieve a "normal" family state. But Christians who place their hope in God and God alone should take heart. Can there be any better place to demonstrate the love and commitment and loyalty of God to the world?

As American culture becomes more and more affluent and self-centered, as long-term relationships become uncommon, as people see one another as expendable, what an opportunity to contrast failing human love with families that hang tough even though they literally could get by without each other. Stepfamilies can set the stage for a new "normal"—that of unconditional acceptance and perpetual openness to restoring relationship.

God—the owner of the cattle on a thousand hills—does not *need* our love or works or companionship. He could literally get by without us. But he *wants* relationship with humanity. He wanted to be rightly related to his creation so badly that he opened the door for people through his Son, Jesus Christ.

If we conform our desires for our families and stepfamilies to God's desires for humankind, we will want relationship with other family members. Even if certain relationships seem awkward, believers committed to God's way will recognize the value in each person God has placed in their lives. And as we change our perspective in the name of Christ before an unbelieving nation, we will surely make God's love look good—as indeed it is!

I believe Christian stepfamilies today can be powerful testimonies during a precarious era for the family. Some images from parables as well as the stories of imperfect families in Scripture provide principles that (1) fan the flame of hope, (2) give parents knowledge and ability to rightly respond, and (3) help them make the best use of everything.

The Principle of Openness: A Father's Initiative

Barbara LeBey, in her book *Family Estrangements,* tells the story of a divorced man, Joe, whose sons refused contact with him. For many years Joe attempted to maintain a relationship with his sons, but to no avail. Losing all hope, Joe sought counseling, which helped him understand his emotions and the forces that stood in the way of his relationship with his sons. Joe moved on with his life and remarried.

After several years of his remarriage, the younger son (then in college) finally made contact. They went into therapy together to work out their problems. Then Joe began new attempts to reunite with the older son, who rejected Joe repeatedly. Finally

Joe chose to attempt a more comfortable approach and invited the son to play golf. The son accepted, to Joe's surprise. Soon they entered a golf tournament and came in second. Never did Joe attempt to talk about the past; he just enjoyed being with his son. After the tournament, Joe's son approached him in the parking lot, hugged him, and said, "I love you, Dad."[1]

LeBey goes on to say that Joe's repeated attempts to mend the relationship greatly improved his chances for restoration. Inwardly Joe did not enjoy the repeated rejection he received.[2] But in spite of his deep hurt, Joe forced himself to behave in a way that showed he was open to restoring relationship with his sons.

One parable in Scripture speaks to that principle of "openness"—the parable of the prodigal son (Luke 15:1–32). Jesus tells this story as the last in a series of three illustrations of God's endless seeking to restore relationship with each and every sinner. The parables of the lost sheep, the lost coin, and the wayward son each demonstrate the initiative taken by the person who suffered the loss to regain what was lost. This is not surprising in the first two parables—a sheep has no capacity to seek out its shepherd, and a coin has no capacity to find its owner.

The last parable strikes a personal nerve for me. A father, when approached with a painful demand by his second son, gives in to the demand. The son wants his part of the inheritance early. The father knows the results will bring dishonor to his name. He feels his son's contempt. He dreads the mistakes his son will make with his fortune. Yet he grants the request and hopes for the day that his son will return. The way Jesus tells the story implies that the father regularly scanned the horizon for his son's return, because one day the father saw the son coming home "while he was still a long way off" (v. 20). And the father, taking the lead, ran to meet him.

Possibly the son was still "a long way off" in every sense of the word, and only after the father's embrace did the prodigal son's

69

heart truly change. The son, rather than being sorry for wounding his father, might have merely regretted that his plan didn't work. The only place he could turn to for help was home.[3]

For the third parable of the prodigal to truly parallel the first two (the lost sheep and the lost coin), it must be understood that the son had no real desire or power to restore relationship with his father. The desire and power to restore belonged to the father, who on his own initiative ran to embrace the son.

Moreover, the father prevented his son from uttering his contrived speech. The openness of the father to restore in spite of past offenses was a tsunami that engulfed them both, making all else petty by comparison. Just as the shepherd rejoiced over finding his one lost sheep, and the woman shouted the good news about finding her lost coin, the father threw a big party to celebrate his son's return.

If only all relationship struggles could end so dramatically and beautifully. They could, if people were perfect. Sadly, though, we all struggle continually with selfish pride and fears, which limit our willingness to risk repeated rejection. The point is, we must maintain the struggle. Every attempt to remain open to family members is a battle won. But both parties lose when Christian parents and stepparents become immobilized by fear and pride, never to engage the struggle.

Does this openness mean believers become doormats? I don't think so. It does mean letting love and grace lead the way in relationships, rather than rules and boundaries. Once the father's love had overwhelmed the son, a new relationship could begin. Had the father greeted his son with "I told you so!" or "How could you be so stupid?" or "If you're going to live under *my* roof, you're going to live by *my* rules!" what chance would there have been for restoration?

Openness means letting go of bitterness and grudges for past offenses. It means making sure the other person knows you desire a real relationship. It means not shutting the other person down when he or she takes those baby steps to restore relationship. It means focusing on the positive steps each person takes to make the relationship stronger, and talking about, but not dwelling on, the behaviors that don't.

The Principle of God's Providence: Abraham's Legacy

No families in Scripture better depict stepfamily struggles than those who descended from Abraham, the father of faith. God ordained that through Abraham would come the nation of Israel, and ultimately the Savior of the world. No matter what Abraham and Sarah did, no matter what their children, grandchildren, or great-grandchildren did, no matter the additional sufferings they brought upon themselves, God's promise and God's plan would be fulfilled.

Abraham, Sarah, and Isaac

Abraham was a remarkable man of faith. At the age of seventy-five, he heard and obeyed God's instructions to pack up his family, his herds, his servants, and all that he owned to move to some undisclosed location (Gen. 12:1–4). When he arrived in Canaan, God told him, "This is the place. The nation that comes from you will dwell here" (v. 7, author's paraphrase). Abraham trusted God's word and built an altar to remind him that God made him a promise.

Abraham sought God's help at Bethel (Gen. 13:4). He proved himself to be a wise man and a pursuer of peace when to avoid a family dispute he gave his nephew Lot the first choice of land in which to settle their respective families and servants (13:8–18). He proved his loyalty to his family when he rescued Lot from the four kings who overtook Sodom and Gomorrah (14:15). His integrity

71

shined when he refused to take gifts from the king of Sodom (14:22). In his old age, Abraham believed God's promise that he would have a son, from whom a nation would be born (15:6).

Time and time again Abraham demonstrated his dependence on God and his desire to be a righteous man (see Gen. 17:23; 18:24; 21:8–13; 22:1–4; 24:6–9).

But Abraham was not a man of perfect faith. Twice Scripture records incidents where Abraham introduced Sarah as his sister and not his wife. Because she was so beautiful, he believed that the kings would kill him to make Sarah their own wife. The Egyptian pharaoh even took her into his own palace before God intervened (12:10–20). But Abraham didn't learn much from that lesson. He did it again in Genesis 20 with King Abimelech, with similar results.

Abraham complicated his and Sarah's life when he agreed to sleep with Hagar in order to get a son. At this point the same jealousies and heartaches that stepfamilies experience entered his life to stay. Hagar "despised" Sarah, and Sarah felt threatened by Hagar and Ishmael. When Sarah died, Abraham remarried and had many more sons. They too were given gifts and cast out of Abraham's home, so that Isaac could be the sole heir to all of Abraham's possessions (see Gen. 16:1–5; 21:8–18).

In our stepfamilies today, that "outsider" status is not deliberate, so much as it is just the way things are. We wish we could love each family member equally, but the battle to achieve that kind of love and belonging never seems to end. Just as it was for Abraham and Sarah, so it is with us. God does not will the pain of family estrangements, but still he can use them to accomplish his purpose.

Isaac, Rebekah, Esau, and Jacob

Isaac and Rebekah appear to have had a monogamous marriage. Scripture does not mention that Isaac had any wives other than Rebekah, nor are any children mentioned other than those born to Rebekah. But their relationship was not without some serious problems. On a slightly humorous note, at least one of the father's sins got passed on to the son. Just as Abraham lied about Sarah, Isaac also introduced Rebekah as his sister to King Abimelech because he feared for his own life (Gen. 26:7–9). King Abimelech must have become pretty disgusted with this family!

On a more serious note, Isaac and Rebekah each had a problem with favoritism, and Esau suffered the brunt of their defects. Isaac favored his firstborn son Esau, but Rebekah loved Jacob more (Gen. 25:28).

When Isaac grew old and blind and was about to die, Rebekah schemed to deceive her husband, disguising Jacob as Esau in order to get him the blessing and the inheritance. Scripture records the raw emotions of both Isaac and Esau when they realized they had been deceived:

His father Isaac asked him, "Who are you?"

"I am your son," he answered, "your firstborn, Esau."

Isaac trembled violently and said, "Who was it, then, that hunted game and brought it to me? I ate it just before you came and I blessed him—and indeed he will be blessed!"

When Esau heard his father's words, he burst out with a loud and bitter cry and said to his father, "Bless me—me too, my father!"

But he said, "Your brother came deceitfully and took your blessing."

Esau said, "Isn't he rightly named Jacob? He has deceived me these two times: He took my birthright, and now he's taken my blessing!" Then he asked, "Haven't you reserved any blessing for me?"

Isaac answered Esau, "I have made him lord over you and have made all his relatives his servants, and I have sustained him with grain and new wine. So what can I possibly do for you, my son?"

Esau said to his father, "Do you have only one blessing, my father? Bless me too, my father!" Then Esau wept aloud.

Genesis 27:32–38

Esau held a grudge against Jacob because of the blessing Jacob stole. Esau said to himself, "The days of mourning for my father are near; then I will kill my brother Jacob" (v. 41).

Esau kept trying to regain his father's approval. When he realized how he had displeased his parents by taking wives from the Canaanites, he took a third wife from Ishmael's family to try to make up for it (28:6–9). But nothing Esau attempted could recover the lost blessing or the approval of his parents.

How many of us are like Esau and can understand the pain of trying to win the approval of those who cannot or will not accept us as we are? Yet as it was with Esau, so it is with us. God did not will the pain of unfair treatment, yet he worked through it all to accomplish his plan.

Jacob and His Sons

Jacob's situation is the most convoluted of all, as we read in Genesis 30. He worked seven years for the woman of his dreams, only to find he'd been tricked. Laban needed to marry off two daughters. Jacob thought he was working for the younger of the two (Rachel) and on his wedding night received the shock of his life. He had married Leah.

Honor required him to keep Leah and to work another seven years for Rachel. God had compassion on Leah, who was not loved by Jacob, and she quickly bore four sons for Jacob. The sisters competed for Jacob's favor, and, like their grandmother-in-law Sarah, offered their maidservants to Jacob to up the baby tally in each column. Jacob did not refuse.

Rachel, who was still Jacob's favorite wife, wanted to borrow some food from Leah. Leah felt Rachel had stolen her husband's affections and resented that Rachel now wanted her food. So Rachel traded her bed in Jacob's tent for food. As a result, Leah bore more children. In total she gave birth to six sons and one daughter, but Rachel was still barren. Finally God heard Rachel's prayers, and she became pregnant with her first child—a boy, Joseph. Later, Rachel died when giving birth to her second child, Benjamin.

The favoritism curse from Isaac and Rebekah continued when Jacob favored his firstborn of Rachel more than all the others (Genesis 37). Joseph's jealous brothers plotted to kill him. One brother, Reuben, had a conscience and could not follow through. That did not prevent the others from selling Joseph into slavery and representing him as dead to their father. But at the end of Genesis, we find that God made it all work for good (chap. 50).

The providence of God cannot be stopped. However, we can make choices out of jealousy, impatience, favoritism, faithlessness, and fear that make the journey much more troublesome. Abraham's fear, Sarah's and Rebekah's impatience, Rachel's and Leah's rivalry, the deception of Joseph's brothers—all created unnecessary hassles, detours, and brokenness along the way because their eyes were on the moment, not God's promises.

At the end of Genesis, Joseph patiently allowed himself to be moved along by God's providence, and he made the best of every situation. He did not try to control people but instead took advantage of opportunities to be an influence. In spite of Joseph's time of slavery (which the stepfamily can seem to be), and in spite of his being falsely accused of a crime (which stepfamily members sometimes are), he helped people wherever he was and ultimately achieved a level of respect and influence that few have ever attained.

God's providence works in every life, and he has a purpose for placing people in specific roles—even stepparents and stepkids. I make the biggest difference not when I focus on fixing people around me or on my plight but when I rest in his plan. I long to be guided by him and avoid the hurtful detours. I also long for the day that I will see completely how he somehow turned the pain I generated, as well as the pain I suffered, into something that worked for someone's good—maybe even my own.

The Principle of Proactive Kindness: Keeping the Covenant

"Wealthy business owner hires a young and gifted protégé who strives to faithfully serve the owner while developing a strong bond with owner's son. Owner's misguided suspicions of protégé's intentions begin a long family legacy of murder and deception, loyalty and betrayal, and bitter, bloody battles ending tragically for all."

This brief synopsis sounds like it could belong to any number of movies, books, or television programs. It also describes the tragic life of David. His tightrope existence as "a man after God's own heart" brought him great drama and personal loss, along with great glory and opportunity to be one of the most influential and powerful writers of Scripture.

One particular shining moment for David speaks strongly to stepfamilies who want to do their best to make up for the losses their kids have suffered. It began with a covenant promise made at a time when two best friends, Jonathan and David, realized that Jonathan's life was at risk because of his loyalty to David (1 Sam. 20:12–17).

Jonathan asked David to protect his family members who survived the upcoming battle for the throne. In the events that transpired to place David on the throne of Israel and Judah, many people in the house of Saul were slaughtered. Jonathan's young son Mephibosheth escaped death because his nurse fled with him before he could be killed.

David later remembered his promise to care for Jonathan's surviving family. David sought out Mephibosheth in order to honor that promise. "Don't be afraid, . . . for I will surely show you kindness for the sake of your father Jonathan. I will restore to you all the land that belonged to your grandfather Saul, and you will always eat at my table" (2 Sam. 9:7).

"I will surely show you kindness. You will always eat at my table." These beautiful words offer restitution but at the same time humbly recognize that no offering can atone for the loss of a boy's father. These beautiful words were not because of any kinship or bond with the son, but because of David's covenant with Jonathan. David never revoked that promise, in spite of possible treason committed by Mephibosheth against him (2 Sam. 16:1–4; 19:24–30; 21:7). David's promise was right to make and right to keep.

What if stepfamily couples made a similar covenant of kindness with regard to each other's children? How often, I wonder, do remarried couples express their devotion to each other by choosing to welcome a stepchild, regardless of the child's response? What if, instead of tiptoeing around the emotions of wounded children or becoming overly critical, stepparents actively demonstrate caring concern and acceptance?

What if parents and stepparents acknowledge the losses their kids have suffered that cannot be fully restored? Then what if they promise from this point forward to become responsible with their lives and their feelings, and to make the best use of everything? Then, as a part of keeping covenant with their spouses, they invest themselves by providing emotional support and stability for each child. The short-term may still be difficult, but what would happen for the child over time?

"I will always show you kindness. You will always eat at my table." Can stepparents do any less, or any more?

The Principle of Faith: Jesus Had a Stepdad

Maybe you have wondered by now, "Aren't there any stepfamilies like mine in the Bible?" While I was hard-pressed to find a family in Scripture that matches the majority of twenty-first-century stepfamilies, one detail took me down an exciting path.

The only biblical record of someone marrying into the role of a parent occurred in the family of Jesus himself. Jesus had a stepdad. Joseph married a single pregnant woman, knowing the child was not his. In faith he followed the instructions of an angel, taking Mary to be his wife, and taking on the responsibility to be an earthly parent to the Savior of the world.

The next logical thought is, *Well, that's completely different! Jesus never sinned, so how hard could that have been?* But Joseph didn't know that at the time he chose to believe the angel. The angel never said, "He'll be perfect . . . literally!"

Joseph knew only that the child in Mary's womb had been miraculously conceived, and that through the child salvation would come, and that he, Joseph, a lowly carpenter, had been asked to take this miracle child and be the best father he could be. While Joseph could have avoided the gossip and suspicions of others or shaken off the angel's visit as merely a dream, he didn't. He got up the next morning and took Mary home to be his wife, allowing her to remain a virgin until after Jesus' birth.

Imagine the pressure of that situation. First of all (even worse than the cases of modern-day remarriages where children are involved), Mary and Joseph had no honeymoon. No weekend on the Galilee coast. No romantic night at Bethlehem Bed and Breakfast. He took his bride home, waited months for the child to be born, and after becoming parents they finally consummated their marriage.

Second, Joseph must have had doubts. If Abraham, the father of faith, couldn't keep from meddling with God's perfect plan, how in the world would Joseph keep from messing up the life of the Son of God? How many times might Joseph have doubted his dreams and wondered if an angel had really visited him? If the angel wasn't real, whose baby was this really? Imagining what Joseph must have been through emotionally gives me hope for the emotional teeter-totter I find myself on as a stepparent.

Third, how exactly would one parent the Son of God? Shouldn't God's Son already know right from wrong? Yet Joseph took action like a typical father. Jesus, at age twelve, became separated from his parents at the Passover feast. When Joseph and Mary found Jesus, Mary said to him, "Son, why have you treated us like this? Your father and I have been *anxiously* searching for you" (Luke 2:48, emphasis added).

Joseph taught Jesus the trade of carpentry; Mark 6:3 records how Jesus' hometown crowd marveled at his wisdom, saying, "Isn't this the carpenter?" Once again, knowing that Joseph felt responsibility toward his "stepson" and trained him to be a competent, contributing member of society gives me encouragement to be a responsible person in the lives of my own stepdaughters.

If Jesus, a perfect man who had a perfect Father, needed training and influence from an *imperfect* stepfather, how much more can imperfect kids with imperfect parents benefit from also having imperfect stepparents who care?

Joseph's obedience was an act of faith. Stepparents and parents must trust that their reasonable act of obedience is to care and be involved. Kids need good role models. By faith, God will use you.

Stepfamilies: Fertile Ground for God's Redemption

The Bible, from beginning to end, is a story about families—family units, lineages of families, and ultimately God's own family as he worked out his plan to redeem a fallen world. In the Christian stepfamily, where so many hurts and disappointments are experienced, couples can be confident that God's grace can abound. Just one person in a family can make a big difference. Rahab's faith in Joshua 6:23 saved the physical lives of her whole family. Lydia brought the gospel message to her family, and all of them received eternal life (Acts 16:15), as did the jailer and his family in Acts 16:33. Believers in stepfamilies have the same awesome opportunity to become agents of grace and redemption.

Check Your Vision

1. How do you believe God wants to use you in your stepfamily?
2. What actions can you take to demonstrate openness to relationship with all of your stepfamily members?
3. What hurts and disappointments have you and members of your stepfamily experienced? Have you seen God's grace abound in spite of the hurts? If so, journal your observations so you don't forget. If not, begin to consciously look for areas where God might be working, and be blessed by joining him in that effort.
4. If spouses choose to welcome each other's children no matter what, what difference do you feel it could make in their marriage? In their family dynamics?

6

The Normal
Stepfamily

*Why Stepfamilies Can't
Go Nuclear*

I once had my portrait made at Glamour Shots. They styled my hair and covered all my flaws with a quarter inch of makeup. I picked out clothes I would never wear in public, and then the consultant "accessorized" me with costume jewelry. I looked great! But it wasn't really me.

Our culture likes to play dress up. We don't like to look at our defects, so we often color our world with more positive slants to avoid having to clean up any negative traits. People are not drunks, they are sobriety impaired; they are not poor, but rather income challenged.

Pop-psychology buzzwords often enter general usage and cause beliefs or reactions in society that actually are not supported by experts. The self-esteem movement is one example. In the same way, common symbols or buzzwords of stepfamily life can create some false ideas in remarried couples.

Consider the modern labels assigned to stepfamilies. First of all, *blended family* seems overly optimistic. It suggests that parts of two different biological families join to make something whole—an outcome that may never take place. *Blended family* implies that random ingredients of diverse backgrounds and flavors get dumped into the same household. Then someone pushes a few buttons. Puree, chop, grate, whip, blend, and voilá! Out comes a smooth and creamy mixture that brings delight to all. More often, the ingredients in the blender behave like oil and vinegar; a true blend cannot happen.

Another term, although not so popular, is *fused family*. This label may or may not fit, depending on what is meant by *fused*. One of Webster's definitions describes it as "blending thoroughly by the process of melting." Another states that fusing is "the merging of diverse, distinctive elements into a unified whole."[1] The "melting" and "merging" definitions work, but to say fused families become a "unified whole" or "blended thoroughly" would be a huge stretch.

The more fitting metaphor for the fused family would be one that's equipped with "a mechanical or electrical detonating device for setting off the bursting charge of a projectile, bomb, or torpedo."[2] Sounds overblown, but sometimes it hits pretty close to home.

Other metaphors that come to mind to describe the stepfamily experience would be things like:

- Shifting sands—you can never be certain of your footing.
- Bumper cars—at first it's a fun ride, but the longer it lasts, the more personal it becomes.

Of course, neither of those labels is very catchy or politically correct.

However, one metaphor that works well has to do with the earth's stability—seismic activity. On the surface things may appear stable, but deep beneath the surface intense pressures work their way up slowly but surely, and many times dramatically.

One part of seismic studies is called plate tectonics. Webster's defines *tectonics* as "a branch of geology concerned with the structure of the crust of a planet, and especially with the formation of folds and faults in it."[3] A label like *tectonic family* conveys an awesome potential for either positive or negative outcomes. It depicts complexity—something we strive to understand but can never master or control. It connotes subsurface frictions, tensions, and activity, varying in degrees of stability, yet able to produce some grand formations.

Its Greek origin, *tekton,* meaning "builder," reminds me that stepfamilies are built steadily over time. They are not labeled "comes completely assembled." Nor do they come with only "some assembly required." Rather, the stepfamily needs well-thought-out blueprints, labor and materials estimates, construction specifications, regular maintenance, and help from experienced people.

The tectonic analogy will likely break down at some point, and maybe it isn't as catchy as "blended" or "fused." Nevertheless, it creates a stepfamily image that includes hope for great things, but with a healthy awareness of the balance and intentional efforts needed to avert disaster.

What makes the stepfamily so much more volatile than the nuclear family? By comparing snapshots of the traditional family with snapshots of the stepfamily, several key differences that undermine stepfamilies become obvious.

Circumstances of Formation

Consider the circumstances surrounding first marriages, compared to those of remarriages. I remember how my first marriage was launched. Our families and friends supported us. Some may have harbored doubts, but if they did, we didn't know it. My father gave us the traditional "marriage is serious business" talk. My mother put people I didn't know on the guest list.

Many showers and gifts came our way, some very touching and meaningful. I particularly remember a little crystal basket given to us by a precious elderly couple who were longtime friends of my fiancé's family. That basket had been given to them when they married more than fifty years before. We married in a beautiful chapel with a pipe organ, and my fiancé's father presided over our vows along with two of his longtime preacher friends. That wedding symbolized a rite of passage, where we separated from our families of origin to become one in marriage—and joy and celebration were the order of the day.

In contrast, the remarriage setting consists of joy in the midst of heartache and insecurities. Stepfamilies form in one of three ways—none of them positive. First, widowhood followed by remarriage, in which all of the emotional struggles of grief become a part of the marital picture. The new generation came into being before the remarried couple was a couple. Prior to the changes in divorce law, stepfamilies almost always formed because of the death of a spouse and the remarriage of the surviving spouse.

The second way in which a stepfamily forms is the one most familiar to our time: divorce followed by remarriage of one or both parties. My second marriage fits this scenario. Five years after my divorce, and about two years after Carl's, we met, fell in love, and got married. "Forsaking all others" and cleaving only to me, his new wife, was not an option available to Carl. He had had two daughters with his previous wife. That relationship could not be completely severed, because they have mutual children; she would be involved in our lives indefinitely.

Hurts and attitudes we accumulated in our first wrecked marriages attached themselves to our new situation. We also were bound to his divorce settlement regarding child custody and support. Decisions about how we would spend portions of our time and money were made before we ever even met.

As for the wedding itself, everyone had mixed emotions. At the time we announced our engagement, the church choir we both sang in was so worried they did something I'd never seen before and haven't seen since. They set aside the end of a rehearsal in order to lay hands on us and pray a very long, sincere prayer for God's protection and blessing—a prayer for which I am very grateful today.

We married in my apartment clubhouse with a much smaller crowd. Looming over the day's joyful events were some foreboding questions: "What if we don't make it?" "What if we're making another mistake?" The atmosphere of celebration, joy, and wholehearted support experienced with a first marriage cannot be quite as full for remarriages.

Children of prior marriages may struggle with both extremes of emotion. Anger over the preventable breakup of their mom and dad may overshadow any excitement about the wedding or the new person in their lives. Children also may be forced to make changes they don't want: new authority figures in their lives, new relatives, less time with the nonresident parent. None of this turmoil exists with first marriages and nuclear families that remain intact.

A third stepfamily type occurs when a man marries a never-married mother. While without the intense emotional swings of divorce and remarriage, this third arrangement still evokes a skeptical joy. The couple, their families, and friends are thrilled to form a complete family but recognize the challenges of less-than-ideal circumstances. Many difficult changes take place at once. The previously single man is suddenly a full-time husband and parent, the mother's time is suddenly divided between a husband and her children, and the children who never had a father suddenly have one.

First marriages require adjustments as well, but stepfamilies do not happen without the members suffering pain, loss, grief, or anger and typically a greater degree of adjustment. Additionally, the members of the new stepfamily often have different perspectives on family relationships than do members of intact families. Children of intact homes feel safe in solid family relationships and fear being alone. Children of remarried families often resist bonding to prevent being hurt, should history repeat itself.[4] These strong fears and other emotions emerge as agents of destruction. Stepchildren naturally respond to conflict and insecurity by acting out negative behaviors—a real threat to stepfamily stability.[5]

The Relationship Phenomenon: "To Infinity and Beyond"

A second reason for instability is the immediate, inflated number of relationships that form from remarriages. As with a front-seat air bag that explodes on impact, after a remarriage each stepfamily member gets slapped in the face with new relationships that often are unwanted.

In intact families, children are gradually added to the mix. Bonds become established between parent and child long before the next child arrives—in nine-month intervals at the least. In an intact family of four, potentially six one-on-one relationships form over time:

- Mom/Dad
- Mom/Child 1
- Mom/Child 2
- Dad/Child 1
- Dad/Child 2
- Child 1/Child 2

If two families of four members each split and remarry, think about the melee caused by these *instantly formed* relationships.

(For the sake of keeping the biological family identities straight, I will use *A* names for one former family unit: Alice, Al, Adam, and Abigail; and *B* names for the second former family unit: Bob, Betty, Brian, and Buffy):

- Mom Alice remarries Dad Bob
- Mom Alice/Her former husband Al
- Mom Alice/Bob's former wife Betty
- Mom Alice/Son Adam
- Mom Alice/Daughter Abigail
- Mom Alice/Stepson Brian
- Mom Alice/Stepdaughter Buffy
- Dad Bob/Former wife Betty
- Dad Bob/Alice's former husband Al
- Dad Bob/Stepson Adam
- Dad Bob/Stepdaughter Abigail
- Dad Bob/Son Brian
- Dad Bob/Daughter Buffy
- Adam/Abigail
- Adam/Brian
- Adam/Buffy
- Brian/Buffy
- Brian/Mom Betty
- Buffy/Mom Betty
- Al/Adam
- Al/Abigail

In this scenario, twenty-one relationships form when one parent remarries. If the other parents also remarry (Betty marries Calvin, and Al marries Doris), another eight relationships get added to that:

- Betty/Calvin
- Calvin/Brian
- Calvin/Buffy
- Al/Doris
- Doris/Adam
- Doris/Abigail
- Bob/Calvin
- Alice/Doris

Now there are six total adults involved (Alice and Bob, Betty and Calvin, Al and Doris). For a really mind-boggling moment, assume all of *their* parents are still alive, which adds twelve in-laws/grandparents to the mix. Then what if Calvin and Doris have children from prior marriages? What if Alice and Bob, Betty and Calvin, and Al and Doris each produce their own children? Can you imagine what Thanksgiving and Christmas must be like, trying to make sure all of the correct grandchildren and step-grandchildren make it to the six homes of all the correct grandparents and step-grandparents? This mix-and-match frenzy was never portrayed in any episode of *The Brady Bunch*, in *Step by Step*, or in the old movie *Yours, Mine, and Ours*.

More relationships mean more relationships in which conflict can occur. More relationships combined with guilt, blame, and resentment left over from the divorce are the formula for "dangerous liaisons" to develop. Experts who study families have discovered one very destructive pattern of relationship they label "triangulation." Two or more family members join forces against a third family member. Research shows that harmful triangles form in stepfamilies more often than in nuclear families.[6]

The stronger bonds of intact families enable members to feel secure in their relationships. The lack of bonding in stepfamilies causes insecurity, mistrust, and thus protective behaviors and high levels of tension and conflict.

Nuclear families are often able to adhere to the K.I.S.S. principle (keep it simple, stupid). Stepfamilies cannot.

Identity Crisis

Everyone performs a number of roles in life—both in the family and outside it. Outside the home, we might become students, coworkers, friends, neighbors, teammates, or many other roles. But family roles, even in nuclear families, often are the hardest to perform well, mainly because they are much more permanent than those outside the home. We can freely change our identities outside the family, but inside the family we are stuck with who we are to each person.

The more permanent identities we have, the more work there is to do to live up to them. Consider the increased identity possibilities within the stepfamily compared to the identities in a nuclear family:

Nuclear Family Identities	Stepfamily Identities
Wife/Mom	Wife/Mom/Stepmom/Ex-wife/The "new" wife
Husband/Dad	Husband/Dad/Stepdad/Ex-husband/The "new" husband
Daughter/Sister	Daughter/Sister/Stepdaughter/Stepsister/Half-sister
Son/Brother	Son/Brother/Stepson/Stepbrother/Half-brother

Children must adjust to new roles and usually a new status as well. The once-oldest child with the most responsibility might become a less-honored middle child in a stepfamily. The child that used to be the precious baby of the family might become a lesser-noticed middle child.

Adults in the stepfamily always take on at least one new role. The children likely will take on three new roles. Adults have the major task of learning how to relate to their stepchildren. Children have the major tasks of learning to relate to their stepparents plus learning to relate to their stepbrothers and stepsisters, half-brothers and half-sisters, and the changing relationship between their divorced mom and dad. The greater adjustment burden is placed upon those least equipped to handle physical and emotional changes.

Social Norms for Stepfamilies

One issue that adds stress to all members of a stepfamily is that no one has defined the proper etiquette for stepfamily interaction. No social norms exist for how the new spouse should relate to the prior spouse. Should they become friends if possible? Should they remain distant? Are they technically relatives or acquaintances, or is it best for them to ignore each other? When I began to realize my husband's former wife would always be in our lives, I started referring to her in a lighthearted manner as "your other wife." This title helped me accept (and even laugh a little at) the difficult truth that I had joined a family already in existence. But after thirteen years, I still am unsure as to the relationship I should have with her.

What about stepgrandparents? Should they expect the same relationship from their stepgrandchildren as they have with grandchildren? Usually the stepgrandparents will remember the stepchild's birthday. Should the stepchild remember theirs? We want our kids to learn to make other people feel special, but is it fair to add a whole new list of relatives that we need to acknowledge on each holiday as "special"?

Or how about the role of the nonresidential parent (usually the father)? Ideally the father will be an equal partner in raising his kids. Legal authorities and some mothers consider fathers to fulfill their fatherly duties as long as the child-support check is on time each month and they make the majority of their visitations.

In order to avoid further conflict, the other parent acquiesces to that position.

Carl fell into this trap. He spent many years feeling forced out of the loop with regard to his children. He deeply resented his lack of control over how his child support was spent and consequently was reluctant to spend additional money on the girls when they came for visitations. He feared confrontation with his former wife, and rather than trying to improve his skills at conflict resolution in order to have more input, he suffered under the control of bitterness until his youngest was nearly out of high school.

In the same way, many nonresidential parents feel put out of their children's lives. It is a difficult situation to resolve, because one parent no longer lives with a child. How can that parent truly parent that child? On top of the sheer logistics, fathers (or mothers) who lose custody often suffer serious emotional wounds. How can they be what their children need in the midst of the intense pain of loss of custody?

Staying involved with children can be emotionally taxing, especially when a hostile relationship exists with the ex-spouse. Often, noncustodial parents settle into merely meeting society's lowest standards and leave it at that.

What about stepparents and stepchildren? Are stepparents supposed to be another parent in the lives of their stepchildren? Should they just be friends? Counselors? Supervisors? Watchdogs? Unpaid, live-in nannies?

Norms for step relationships don't exist, and likely they never will. So many factors influence the possibilities for each relationship: the circumstances of the divorce, how the children receive the new circumstances, the quality of communication among members, the frequency of visits, the ages of the children, the maturity of the adults, and hundreds of other variables.

Then when stepparents figure out the possibilities for their own family, they still don't feel confident enough to trust them.

No two stepparents travel an identical journey. Each must forge his or her own path.

The Sane Step: Pitfalls to Avoid

Few new stepparents understand the intensity of the emotional tug-of-war of stepfamily life. Like a woman in childbirth, we knew it would hurt, but not this bad or this long! Taking on the issues of three families—the two previous homes of origin plus the new struggles of the new stepfamily—seems an insane proposition. Yet it is a noble one when we remember that God is a Redeemer and a Rebuilder, and he is involving us in his plan to restore wounded hearts. So what are some of the insanity traps of stepfamily life that stepparents can work to avoid so we do not go insane in the process?

Trapdoor #1: Feeling like a Failure

Since no one goes to stepparent school, we each go through on-the-job training. Stepfamily research provides some framework. But the framework is not completely stable, because the foundation of the stepfamily, by its very nature, is unstable.

In my own experience, my role evolved based upon the developmental needs and emotional states of my stepdaughters. I was usually slow to realize when things were changing, which added to the stress. While they were young, they accepted me willingly as a friendly parent and authority figure. As they grew older, they began to see me as a peer and sometimes a mentor. In their teen years, they have realized that they can choose the kind of relationship we will have; they have the freedom to remain connected or to disconnect.

Does this cause me frustration? Yes. I go through a grief process every time things change for the worse, and I must overcome the fear of repeated rejection when it seems as if things are turning around. The spirit of a sound mind tells me to accept with thankfulness the good they can offer and to be content with whatever right I can do.

Stepfamilies that work to agree on the stepparent's role can experience an easier adjustment to stepfamily life.[7] I believe that they will also benefit from fine-tuning the agreement as the children grow, as their needs change, and as they come to deeper levels of understanding about their family situation.

Trapdoor #2: Lack of Unity in Discipline Efforts

In his book *The Smart Stepfamily,* Ron Deal states:

> Stress in a stepfamily generally divides people along biological lines. When push comes to shove, the allegiance (or loyalty) between parents and children often wins out over the marriage unless the couple can form a unified position of leadership. If they cannot govern the family as a team, the household is headed for anger, jealousy, and unacceptance. . . . If a biological parent is not willing to build such a bridge with the stepparent, the stepchildren will receive an unhealthy amount of power in the home.[8]

Children will believe that they have control of their parent's heartstrings and that they will be the uncontested winners when a parent is forced to choose between them and the new spouse. They also believe that their bad behaviors can create a wedge between parents and stepparents. Lecturing, losing control, and overreacting will only prove their case. Dispelling those beliefs takes time—lots of time. Changing a child's perception takes consistent, gentle, and loving communication from the couple to show that they are united and functioning as a team to manage the family. The divisive behaviors of children may never

93

completely disappear, but the more they subside, the greater everyone's sanity.

Trapdoor #3: A Critical Spirit toward Stepkids and Spouses

To avoid the critical spirit trap with stepkids:

- Offer them your friendship. Show kindness. Laugh together and have fun, but don't use "fun" to escape helping them through hard issues. Be authentic.
- Handle their feelings with tact and dignity. Listen well and affirm their rights to their feelings.
- Model the things you hope they will learn.
- Offer to help them with problems, such as homework and relationships.
- When they solicit your input, answer questions well and unemotionally.
- Discipline them according to the guidelines you and your spouse agreed on and communicated well to the kids.
- Don't give up.

To avoid that trap with your spouse:

- Discuss conflicts *behind closed doors* (where no "big ears" can listen in) and allow your spouse to do the same.
- If there is no mutually agreeable compromise, allow your spouse to make the final call regarding his or her own children, then support that decision.
- Don't be in a hurry to assume an authoritative role with your stepkids.
- Don't give up.

Trapdoor #4: Anger

Anger is a *normal* part of the stepfamily experience. If you can't manage anger well, you'll add fuel to the fire. Some suggestions for anger management include:

- Memorize some of the anger Scriptures:

  A gentle answer turns away wrath,
  But a harsh word stirs up anger.

  Proverbs 15:1 NASB

  But everyone must be quick to hear, slow to speak and slow to anger.

  James 1:19 NASB

  But now you also, put them all aside: anger, wrath, malice, slander, and abusive speech from your mouth.

  Colossians 3:8 NASB

  Be angry, and yet do not sin; do not let the sun go down on your anger, and do not give the devil an opportunity.

  Ephesians 4:26–27 NASB

- Recall the last time you reacted in anger to a stepchild. Note specifically what tripped your angry reaction. Think of several alternative responses that would have been more constructive.
- Pay attention when stepchildren begin to push your emotional buttons. Employ an alternative response rather than "doing what comes naturally."
- Ask questions rather than commenting. A stepparent who encourages a child to talk, and tries to fully under-

stand, will make much more progress than a stepparent who needs to prove his or her "rightness."

- Don't be sucked into power struggles.
- When you feel like exploding, excuse yourself from the situation. Take time to be alone with your emotions, to review the problem, and to plan an honest response that will promote goodwill.

Controlling anger serves several purposes. Children learn by example that emotions can be managed.[9] Also, by not reacting violently, stepparents demonstrate their commitment to working on the relationship. Listening to the stepchild and trying to understand his or her hurts develops compassion and prevents a stepparent from returning a child's angry blows with potshots.

On the Sunny Side . . .

Indeed the portrait of a stepfamily differs greatly from that of a nuclear family. The differences stem from the fracture caused by divorce. Before moving on from this topic, be assured that along with the trials of stepfamily living come wonderful moments. Here are some snapshots that have helped to make it all worthwhile.

- My stepdaughters, Melissa at age eight and Tracy at age six, praying to receive Jesus into their lives—and I was part of it.
- The three of us, watching *The Nutcracker*, running and leaping through the house to "The Dance of the Flowers."
- The thrill of listening to Tracy, who, having returned from a World-changers Mission Trip, told about how she led a little girl to Christ.

- Our family adventure fording the Buffalo River two miles on foot, singing "Climb Every Mountain" until we finally reached the Highway 14 bridge.
- The deep conversations Melissa and I had on drives to and from her mother's house.
- The many hours of laughing together and rehashing classic comedy lines.
- Their graduations from high school.

These moments, among many others, make the journey of my "tectonic family" worthwhile—even priceless!

Check Your Vision

1. List the various roles each member of your stepfamily has within the stepfamily. Which role seems most troublesome for each member? How did the status of each member change when the stepfamily formed?
2. List all of the new, immediate relationships that formed when you became a stepfamily. How have those relationships changed over time?
3. What priceless "tectonic" moments have provided strength and stability for your stepfamily? How can you facilitate more of these positive moments?

7

Weeds from the Past

A Stepfamily's Worst Foe

Carl and I have a small vegetable garden. After four growing seasons of experience, I wish for a method to be weed free. Forever. We just tried lasagna gardening. Theoretically, by layering things like newspaper, compost, grass clippings, chopped leaves, wood ashes, and peat, you can kill off the weeds and sod beneath it all and have a weed-free garden.

I hope that's the case, but history tells me I will forever battle my weeds. Those stubborn roots just won't die, and weed seeds are always floating in from somewhere to land in my nicely prepared soil.

In the same way, divorced Christians usually wish they could just be free of their past. They wish they could forgive and forget quickly and just be content. However, few deeper emotional wounds exist than those that take place in most divorces. Rejection, betrayal, broken trust, deception, and disappointment—all of these seeds produce weeds that flourish to choke out the good plants we want to keep, no matter how many "good things" we try to layer on top.

Sadly, the children are some of the valuable plants that become choked out when divorced parents don't weed regularly or thoroughly. Some of those hard-to-pull roots include bitterness, inadequacies, and guilt. The first step in making your family environment a healthier place to thrive is to recognize the weeds and apply the necessary treatments to control them.

The Weed of Bitterness

See to it that . . . no bitter root grows up to cause trouble and defile many.

Hebrews 12:15

Jerry was ten when his parents divorced. Both of his parents had problems with alcohol, and both contributed to the violent arguments Jerry witnessed over the years. Yet Jerry blamed his mother for chasing his father away, and his anger grew and grew.

Jerry's mother remarried. Her new husband preferred a quiet, orderly household. To keep the peace, Jerry had to jump through lots of behavioral hoops that he felt were unfair. He resented his stepdad, but even more, he resented his mom for accommodating her husband at the expense of her own children.

Jerry grew up and married Jan, who suffered the fruits of Jerry's weeds of anger and resentment. When Jan tired of coping with Jerry's hurt, she filed for divorce, taking Jerry's children away from him. Now two important women in his life had robbed him of special people in his life—his father and his children. He layered bitterness on top of bitterness.

Jerry became a Christian and remarried. He hoped a Christian wife would be different. Initially Jerry agreed they could have kids together, but when the time came and his new wife wanted to try, his bitterness took over. Jerry could not trust his new wife to not reject him as he believed his mother and first wife had done. He feared losing more children to divorce.

Jerry's bitterness soured all his important relationships for many years. His family members knew to move carefully around him, so as not to provoke an episode of anger or depression. Anger blinded him to any good in other people—they were all out to get him or rob him of pleasure.

When anger ceases to be a temporary reaction to an event and becomes an ongoing heart attitude toward a person, or something that frequently arises without good explanation, it is no longer anger but bitterness. Webster's dictionary associates these words with the word *bitter*: "relentlessly determined, intense animosity, harshly reproachful, marked by cynicism and rancor, contempt."[1]

Bitterness not only becomes a way of dealing with the person whom we perceive wronged us, but also shows up in our relationships with anyone whose actions might remind us of that person. It affects more than just our relationships with others. Some pastors and doctors have estimated that potentially 65 to 85 percent of all physical sickness is connected to feelings of hate, bitterness, and resentment.[2] The open emotional wounds serve as constant reminders of the pain that might be experienced if we open up to someone else.

Signs of Bitterness

Sometimes we may not realize when we are carrying bitterness over past experiences. We have left the person or the event that angered us in the past and never realize how many of the choices we make in the present are predicated on that past incident.

For example, from my seventh-grade year through high school, I hung out with the same group of girlfriends. We did almost everything together, but in our senior year, a few of our group members fell into a new crowd. The day of our graduation we tried to plan a place to go celebrate together, but those in the new crowd did not feel like the rest of us would fit in with the place they wanted to go, so they would not invite us along. In my mind, I got over it quickly and moved on. Several years later I was invited to a little reunion with the group. I made an excuse not to go—those people who had rejected me didn't deserve to see me! For years I would not form close friendships with other people because I did not want to be rejected again.

Some manifestations of bitterness in our lives might include:

- An intense dislike of someone we either don't really know or don't have a good reason to dislike
- An overblown reaction to a minor offense
- A general mistrust of the intentions of others
- Scheming and plotting ways to make another person pay for a wrong done or experiencing pleasure when that person is suffering
- An inability to see any good in another person
- An inability to be vulnerable with someone who has proven his or her ability to be trusted
- Avoiding interactions with family members or friends who have hurt us in the past, even after they have sought our forgiveness
- A negative attitude each time we must interact with an individual

Treating Bitterness

Bitterness is not something we can just stop having. Its source is deep-seated. When something happens to trigger it, we can do little to prevent the initial emotions that surface. But we can learn to recognize them when they happen and disable them before they damage present relationships.

In his book *Victory over the Darkness,* Neil T. Anderson gives a complete list of instructions for treating the bitter weeds in our hearts. He offers two basic steps.

Step 1: Begin to look at your past in light of who you really are. He states, "Remember, your emotions are a product of how you perceived the event, not the event itself. Refuse to believe that you are just the product of your past experiences. As a Christian, you are primarily a work of Christ on the cross."[3] We can choose to stop believing our feelings and start believing that Christ has set us free from the things in our past.

Step 2: Forgive. This is, of course, the hardest step of all. We must choose to stop punishing those who have hurt us in the past. Anderson states, "In reality, you will have to live with the consequences of the offender's sin whether you forgive him or not. . . . You can either choose to live in bitterness and unforgiveness or in peace and forgiveness by deciding not to use the offense against him. The latter, of course, is God's way."[4] Here are some steps he suggests to move toward forgiveness:

- Make a list of those who have offended you, and describe the wrongs you have suffered.
- Acknowledge the pain you have suffered. Write down how you really feel about the offender and what he or she did.
- Acknowledge that Christ died "once for all" (Heb. 10:10).

103

- In light of what Christ did, take that person off your "hit list."
- In prayer, give each offense and each person to God. Tell God you have forgiven him or her. (Keep it between you and God unless that person at some point comes to you seeking forgiveness.)
- Take responsibility for any part you played in the event and ask God for forgiveness. If you are aware that someone has something against you, go to that person and ask forgiveness (Matt. 5:23–26).
- Destroy the list.
- Begin praying for those who have offended you. Allow God to help you understand them.
- Expect God to begin changing your heart toward them, and thank him for growing you more into Christ-likeness.[5]

The Weed of Inadequacy

> Cast your cares on the LORD
> and he will sustain you;
> he will never let the righteous fall.
>
> Psalm 55:22

Lisa and Todd went through a messy divorce four years ago. Lisa remarried last year, and Todd just got remarried. Kathy seemed like a great person—maybe a little too great! Every other weekend, Lisa heard from her kids just how great Kathy was: how great she cooked, how great she was at sports, the great parties she had.

It seemed Kathy was everything Lisa wasn't. She knew the kids loved her, but since they never talked about her the way they talked about Kathy, she began to fear that she was losing them.

Lisa thought it would be good to plan some fun things to do with the kids. Theater tickets to see *The Lion King* just happened to be available only during Todd's weekend, so they would have to skip this visitation. Sometimes she "forgot" to send the right clothes on the daddy weekends. She knew that would probably tick Kathy off and maybe the kids would see that Kathy has bad moods like everyone else. Lisa needed to win some points of her own from her kids and hoped Kathy would teeter off of that pedestal of hers as well.

Divorce means loss—loss of a partner, loss of a dream, possibly a loss of self-respect, loss of relationship with extended family, maybe loss of income and security, and serious blows to our identity. Hard questions wage war on our self-image: "Why?" "What did I do wrong?" "Am I so hard to live with?" "Am I that unlovable?" "How am I going to take care of these kids?" "I wonder if the kids still love me?" After such tremendous loss, we may suddenly feel inadequate and need answers to these questions.

Unfortunately, the way we often try to answer them comes at the expense of others. We need kudos to counteract all those negative thoughts, so we play that old comparison game. Some insidious strategies to win the comparison game include:

- Criticizing the other parent's parenting
- Becoming a people pleaser
- Criticizing the stepparent's caregiving
- Buying a child's affection or loyalty with money or greater leniency in parenting
- Immediately entering a new relationship to prove self-worth
- Justifying wrong behaviors by comparing one's own actions to those who are clearly "worse"

Our identities are formed based on our relationships with people, both past and present.[6] If we are not accepted in a place that is important to us (i.e., family, work, church), we begin to believe what it seems others think about us. We lose sight of who we thought we were. Attacks to our self-image associated with divorce and remarriage will happen, but seeking achievement, recognition, or affection from people is a losing strategy to combat them.

To get out of that insidious comparison and performance trap, a new basis for our identity must be sought. Charles Solomon, author of *The Rejection Syndrome,* suggests answering three important questions to establish an identity that cannot be taken away.[7] The model is found in Matthew 16:13–16, where Jesus asked his disciples two questions: "Who do men say that I am?" and "Who do you say that I am?"

First, honestly and thoroughly answer the question, "Who do people say that you are, or that you should be?" List all the positives and negatives that you perceive others see in you. Their opinions may have been communicated either verbally or nonverbally, and intentionally or unintentionally. Some opinions may have carried more weight than others, and you may have received conflicting messages (i.e., one person may see you as outgoing and another person as shy).

Second, answer the question, "Who do you say that you are?" Do you agree with what others see in you, either in part or in whole? Have you accepted what others think as true and stopped working on an identity of your own?

Third, answer the question, "Who does God say that you are?" This, of course, is the most important question. For believers, God says we are his children (Gal. 4:4–7), we are "in Christ" (1 Cor. 1:30), and we are in the process of becoming all he created us to be (2 Cor. 3:18).

When we give up our worldly basis for identity, whether that is who others say we are or who we think we ought to be, and identify ourselves with Christ, we can escape the performance trap. God is the only one who will always accept us completely, all the time, and in his eyes, we are still "becoming."

In our example, as Lisa understands that God loves and accepts her unconditionally, she can stop jumping through hoops and using manipulation to maintain the love of others. As she finds her life "in Christ," she will realize that the criticisms, persecutions, and rejections she has suffered do not have to affect her meaning and purpose in life, just as those suffered by Christ did not thwart his purpose. As she realizes that God is not finished with her yet, she can rest on her "becoming" identity in Christ, rather than fretting over who she is not to others. As a result, the love and acceptance she does experience from people in her life will not be phony and contrived, but honest and real, the kind of love we truly hunger for.

The Weed of Guilt

> Search me, O God, and know my heart;
>   test me and know my anxious thoughts.
> See if there is any offensive way in me,
>   and lead me in the way everlasting.
>
> Psalm 139:23–24

"Your mom's been nagging me again about the things I let you do when you're with us. So no video games after 10:00, okay?" Al knew he should provide more structure when the kids were at his house, but they enjoyed being with him because he didn't have so many rules. He wanted them to want to come over. He wanted to make up for all the pain he had caused in their lives. He knew his ex-wife had problems getting them back into a routine when they went back to her house, but that was her problem. Al's new wife wanted to enforce the same rules she used for her kids on his kids. On the surface, he agreed with her, but he could not follow through.

Deep down, Al carried guilt over the family breakup, and this guilt went untended. If he did try to enforce a rule, he told his kids it was because their mother or stepmother wanted it that way—it wasn't his fault. Each time he blamed someone else, he planted seeds of rebellion and resentment in his kids. He also created tension in his own home: His stepchildren grew to resent him for favoring his own kids, and his wife felt he undermined her efforts.

Guilt can become a gigantic weed that spawns poisonous fruit if we continue to ignore it. Several feelings we might experience that indicate the presence of guilt are shame, fear of being discovered, fear of consequences for an action, hopelessness, anxiety, defensiveness, or denial ("It wasn't my fault").[8] Guilt can be either true (from God) or false (when the accusation is based on a lie or a false understanding of right and wrong).

True guilt is "a form of mental and emotional pain we experience when we feel responsible for doing, or not doing, something which violates our personal moral standard."[9] It can be a productive tool if handled properly or an unbearable oppression if ignored. If we listen to it and take appropriate steps to deal with it, it can help us grow and strengthen our relationships with others. If we ignore guilt, it starts to produce negative fruits immediately. First comes the fruit of blame, which produces the pollen of resentment. Resentment will infect every plant in the garden.

False guilt comes from things that are not really wrong but somehow we've come to think are wrong. We punish ourselves or accept blame for something that was not ours to carry. We work perpetually to make up for something that cannot be changed. This kind of guilt will always be oppressive and will always lead to resentment.

The first step in dealing with guilt is to be honest in our hearts about the source of the guilt. What was our part, if any, in the wrong that was done? In Al's case, perhaps he did all he could to save his marriage. Perhaps his wife refused to work at the marriage but blamed him for being a poor husband. Al can suffer under false guilt and pay for it the rest of his life or he can realize that it was her choice to end it. Unless Al admits the wrong done to him, he'll ignore his hurt as invalid. He won't acknowledge his true feelings about it and therefore won't see the need to forgive his ex-wife. Without forgiveness, God's grace cannot work in his life.[10]

Or perhaps Al has much reason to feel guilty for the family breakup. An honest acknowledgment of his behaviors that led to the divorce is the first step to breaking the bondage. Guilt will serve as a reminder not to repeat those same behaviors. But he cannot stop there.

The next difficult step is to seek and receive forgiveness (see the steps to forgiveness in this chapter under "Treating Bitterness" on pages 103–104). Al needs to agree with God about his part and receive God's forgiveness; seek it from those he hurt, if appropriate (whether they grant it or not); and then let himself off the hook. He needs to forgive himself. Al needs to understand that if God is not holding anything against him, he has no right to punish himself.

If Al will deal properly with his guilt, whatever its source, he can leave his past in the past and do the job of a responsible parent for his kids in the present. He can stop paying the debt that the Son of God paid on a cross over two thousand years ago. It is finished.

Check Your Vision

1. Are there people in your life who suffer your constant criticism or sense your continual disapproval? To help you locate the source of your feelings, take a legal-sized piece of paper, turn it the long way, and make a chart with five columns:

Column 1: The name of the person you feel
negatively toward

Column 2: How you feel about that person

Column 3: What that person did to cause those
negative feelings

Column 4: (If little to nothing in column 3)
Other person or event in your life
that may have caused your feelings

Column 5: Whom do you need to forgive?

2. In what areas of your life do you feel inadequate? To whom
do you compare yourself? Do you believe God sees you as
inadequate for the responsibilities he has placed in your
life, or has he given you everything you need for life and
godliness?

3. In what areas do you feel compelled to hide mistakes of
the past? To make up for past mistakes? Take these areas
to God in prayer and let him help you deal with your
guilt—whether true or false—once and for all.

8

Weed Killer #1: Cooperative Parenting

Seven Coparenting Be-Attitudes

In her book *The Unexpected Legacy of Divorce,* Judith Wallerstein states, "Ask any child of divorce. In every domain of the child's life, parents are less available and less organized, provide fewer dinners together or even clean clothing and do not always carry out regular household routines or help with homework or offer soothing bedtime rituals."[1] Too focused on personal pain and rebuilding their private lives, many parents never rise above it to provide the support their children need.

Not only do children suffer from diminished parenting, but many are also emotionally torn between parents who cannot cooperate with each other. About 50 percent of remarried spouses fall into the general description of "difficult," and there are several ways to be a difficult former spouse. The "intruder" ex-spouse attempts to control the other family by such tactics as manipulating money, seeking the loyalty of the kids, or not communicating directly. The "chaos creator" threatens and attacks the remarried spouse. The "absentee" parent makes support payments and visitations dependably but becomes emotionally detached from the children. The "abuser" does just that—abuses alcohol or drugs, or possibly becomes physically, emotionally, or sexually abusive to children.[2]

As parents strive to rise above these stereotypes to unite for the purpose of raising their kids, they will see their children thrive. Not only will the kids benefit from cooperative parenting, but the parents will improve their own quality of life as well. Once we understand the destructive impact our emotions can have on parenting and our own quality of life (see chapter 7), we can implement some proactive strategies to guard against their invasions.

This chapter and the two following chapters offer some preemergent treatments to keep our emotional weeds under control. Weed Killer #1: Take the initiative to be a cooperative coparent with your former spouse.

Seven Be-Attitudes for Coparenting

Children can overcome the setbacks caused by their parents' divorce. Those who do, do so primarily because their parents did not use them as weapons to hurt each other and at least one parent continued to nurture them properly.[3] Children appear to do better when (1) they keep in close contact with both parents and (2) the parents cease fighting or never start to fight after the breakup.[4] So when divorced parents find themselves buried in weeds, how can they begin to dig themselves out?

In Matthew 5 Jesus taught nine beatitudes for blessed living. The Amplified Bible translates the word *blessed* as "happy, fortunate, to be envied" (AMP). Several of the nine "Blessed are" statements contradict our typical ideas of things that lead to happiness, such as "blessed are the poor in spirit" (v. 3), or "blessed are those who mourn" (v. 4), or "blessed are those who are persecuted because of righteousness" (v. 10).

The paradox of the Christian life is that often what we least want in our lives can work for our ultimate well-being. With that in mind, consider these seven "Be-attitudes" to pollinate the plants in your coparenting garden and produce healthier kids: be healed, be dependable, be the adult, be respectful, be perceptive, be near, and be a team.

Be Healed

> Heal me, O LORD, and I will be healed;
> save me and I will be saved,
> for you are the one I praise.

Jeremiah 17:14

Confess your sins to each other and pray for each other so that you may be healed.

James 5:16

According to researchers, divorce recovery can take between two and five years but might never take place if the person does not exert effort to recover. If you will be healed, consider taking some of the following steps:

- Read, read, read. Learn about the effects of divorce on adults and children and how to overcome the hurts of the past.
- Write. Journal your own ups and downs. What made you yell at the kids today? Why did that anger toward your ex-spouse rear its ugly head today? What testy situation went better than expected and why? Forcing your-

self to analyze your emotions and reactions will prepare you for the next trial.

- Don't dwell on the past; plan for the future. Who do you want to become? How do you want your kids to grow up? What can you do now to bring those things to pass?
- When in the dumps over your own unmet emotional needs, switch your focus to someone else's emotional need and take action right then to meet it.
- Seek counsel from a pastor or a professional counselor.
- Become part of a Christian support group such as Divorce Recovery.
- Pray. Honestly confess feelings and emotions to God, no matter how ugly they are. (He can handle it!) Seek his comfort and his perspective.

The Explosive Ordinance Disposal units of our U.S. military are brave and selfless soldiers trained to dismantle enemy rockets before they detonate. They must know weapons so well that they can go straight to the critical element of a bomb or a rocket and make it ineffective in a matter of seconds. They risk their lives with each assignment. In the same way, we need to overcome our fear of pain and train ourselves to disable our emotions; yes, for our own safety and security, but even more for that of our children.

Be the Adult

When I was a child, I talked like a child, I thought like a child, I reasoned like a child. When I became a man, I put childish ways behind me.

1 Corinthians 13:11

In other words, "when I grew up, I began to speak as an adult, think as an adult, and reason as an adult." Divorced couples frequently resort to childish ways of dealing with each other. So the first tip for being the adult is to learn to communicate with the other parent in an adult manner.

Do Away with Childish Speaking. To communicate means to transmit information, thought, or feeling so that it is satisfactorily received or understood. Most of us were not overtly taught the ingredients of good communication. We followed the unspoken rules of communication in our family until we were old enough to realize that we liked some methods our family used to communicate and others just got on our nerves.

In some families, methods such as pouting, screaming, the silent treatment, dirty looks, nagging, whining, threats, sarcasm, accusations, and guilt are used to obtain desired behaviors. These, of course, are childish methods that have no place in adult communication. The message might be satisfactorily received and understood as far as the sender is concerned, but the receiver of these messages feels controlled and becomes resentful.

Adult communication recognizes the value in each person's point of view, is not afraid to seek understanding, and makes a genuine effort to meet in the middle. Where ex-spouses are concerned, expect contrasting viewpoints. After all, couples commonly divorce due to "irreconcilable differences." While they no longer have to reach a consensus regarding each other personally, they must, for the sake of the children, commit to reaching a consensus on parenting decisions.

Healthy communication takes time and practice to achieve. Here are some suggestions for speaking like an adult with former spouses:

- Begin conversations by affirming the goal of doing your best together for the kids: "We're here for the sake of the kids."

- Decide to make understanding your goal, rather than trying to persuade your former spouse.

115

- Choose your issues carefully. Be absolutely certain the issue is the child's welfare and not an unhealed wound trying to hurt or control your former spouse.

- Ask questions in a sincere attitude of concern: "What role do you want to play as a parent?" "How do you think we can best handle this situation?" "May I share my point of view?"

- Give your full attention to the other person. Don't plan your response while the other person talks.

- Don't interrupt the other person.

- Avoid blaming and accusing. If it is necessary to address a truly wrong behavior of the other party, use "I" statements: "I've seen this, and it concerns me." "I feel very left out of the decision making."

- Prior to responding, clarify ambiguities to make certain you understood the other person's perspective: "Did I understand you correctly when you said . . . ?" "So from your point of view . . ."

- Treat meetings with your ex as business meetings.

    Have a specific agenda.

    Prepare beforehand.

    Address issues one at a time.

    Allow all parties to calmly state how their area is affected.

    Brainstorm solutions to problems.

    Assign action items.

    End the meeting on schedule.

- Communicate like an adult both verbally and nonverbally, even if the other person doesn't.

If communicating with the former spouse is particularly difficult, consider mediation. Divorced couples who use mediation to design a parenting plan report fewer conflicts, better communication, improved attitudes toward one another as parents, and greater satisfaction with the divorce aftermath than do divorcing couples who remain hostile.[5]

Pray before the meeting and afterward. Before: Ask God to give you wisdom and a right spirit. After: Cast all your after-meeting emotions and cares upon the one who cares passionately for you. Ask him to reveal weaknesses in your communication so that you can improve the next time around.

Do Away with Childish Thinking and Reasoning. The second tip in being the adult is to grow up in our self-talk. Often fear of conflict causes us to deal with issues only inside our own minds. The table below lists some faulty thinking patterns and gives a specific example of each.

Destructive Thinking	Example	Constructive Thinking
Imaginary conversations that vent the full weight of our anger and resentment on those who have hurt us	"It's your fault we got divorced! It's your fault your kids hate you! All you care about is yourself!"	"God, I wish he/she could see how much we've been hurt. Help me not hate. Help me not make this worse."
Rewriting events that took place to put ourselves in a more favorable light	"He/she was the one who started it. Not me! I was only trying to help."	"I pushed his/her buttons again. I'm sorry, Lord. Help me admit my part in this."
Scheming subtle ways to hurt the other person	"I'll just tell little Susan we don't have enough money for ballet since her dad can't pay his child support on time."	"I'll have to tell Susan we'll just save our money and catch the next ballet class."
Excusing our less-than-adult behaviors	"My former spouse has all the power over my kids, so my efforts to parent are pointless. Why try?"	"I know it's hard on my former spouse when I don't make little Joey mind. I'll do better next visit."

Today's media messages also impact parents' thinking. Movies, TV sitcoms, and commercials represent kids as being smarter than their parents and portray parents as killjoys trying to ruin their kids' lives. These outside influences to our thinking and reasoning increase the need for former spouses to unite in their parenting. Here are some suggestions for thinking and reasoning like an adult:

Take every thought captive (2 Cor. 10:5). Feelings of stress or anxiety might indicate some runaway thoughts that need to be reined in. Ask yourself: "Do my thoughts center on my own desires or on my child's well-being?" "Am I angry or at peace? Vindictive or at peace? Bitter or at peace? Pathetic or at peace? Fearful or at peace?" If anything other than peace is going on, test those thoughts and make certain they are being obedient to Christ.

Express those emotional thoughts to God before acting on them or expressing them to someone else. I have written letters to dump my angry thoughts. Whenever I take them to God first, the smoke seems to clear, and I can then precisely communicate my concerns in love rather than in anger.

Confess your thoughts to a trusted and objective friend. Often just saying them out loud and hearing yourself spew is enough to help you see the absurdities of your thinking.

Notice when your thoughts dwell on negative or futile imaginations, and choose to think on things that are pure, true, beautiful, and righteous. Philippians 4:8 says, "*whatever* is right," and "if *anything* is worthy of praise," to think on *these* things (emphasis added).

Children need equal effort from both parents in providing authoritative, mature guidance for their lives. As the old saying goes, "United we stand, divided we fall." Support each other in speaking, thinking, and coparenting like adults.

Be Dependable

Now it is required that those who have been given a trust must prove faithful.

1 Corinthians 4:2

Parents are stewards of the children God has given them, and God holds each steward accountable for their care. Part of maintaining an atmosphere that enables coparenting is faithfulness in all commitments, especially those in the court documents. Children should be able to depend on both of their parents to continue to be parents. To be a dependable parent:

- Fulfill child support obligations in a timely way and without using them to manipulate the other parent. Communicate any changes in payment methods to the other parent so as not to lose his or her trust (i.e., job changes or relocations that will affect how and when child support payments are to be made).
- Respect the court-ordered purpose of the support. Offer to give a periodic account to the other parent of how the funds are used to care for the children.
- Faithfully make visitations.
- Faithfully allow visitations without hassle in any manner.
- Plan regular meetings by phone or in person so that both parents stay informed of issues concerning the child.
- Learn all you can about the effects of divorce and step-family life on children, and take action to alleviate hardships.

Be Respectful

Each of you should look not only to your own interests, but also to the interests of others.

Philippians 2:4

Whenever Rodney Dangerfield said, "I don't get no respect!" he meant, "Nobody cares what I think." Respect basically means to assign value or worth to someone or some idea. Walk into almost any public school classroom, and one of the rules posted

119

for the class and the teachers to follow will be "Respect each other and respect yourself." In other words, value others and value yourself.

After a divorce, valuing the former spouse is often the furthest thought from our minds. But it is something we need to do, because we value our children, because we still have a long-term relationship with their other parent, and because every person has value and worth in God's eyes.

First, respect the need of the children to have the other parent in their lives. Children need both a father and a mother. Changes in divorce law over the past twenty years have recognized a child's need to have strong and ongoing relationships with both parents. Psychological studies indicate that children do best with the ongoing involvement of fathers.[6]

Second, respect the other parent's right to be involved in decisions and events concerning the children. Respect the other parent's opinions. Both parents have many hopes and convictions over what their children should learn and character traits they hope to teach their children. Parents can learn from each other's observations and open each other's eyes to different issues. My former boss used to say, "There is none so smart as all of us." Parents can learn from each other.

Third, respect the fact that parenting is a difficult job no matter the circumstances. All parents make mistakes. But divorced parents are particularly susceptible to finger-pointing and blame (a sign of that "guilt" weed). Ways to demonstrate respect for each other include:

- Keeping a calendar of important dates concerning the kids and copying that calendar for the other parent
- Communicating parenting successes, challenges, and progress to the other parent
- Not speaking negatively to the children about the other parent

- Allowing children the freedom to contact the other parent at will
- Keeping a positive attitude in front of the kids regarding the other parent
- Listening to requests from the other parent and honoring those requests as much as possible
- Allowing emotions to subside before addressing difficult issues with the other parent

Be Perceptive

[Moses'] sister stood at a distance to see what would happen to him.

Then Pharaoh's daughter went down to the Nile to bathe, and her attendants were walking along the river bank. She saw the basket among the reeds and sent her slave girl to get it. She opened it and saw the baby. He was crying, and she felt sorry for him. "This is one of the Hebrew babies," she said.

Then his sister asked Pharaoh's daughter, "Shall I go and get one of the Hebrew women to nurse the baby for you?"

"Yes, go," she answered. And the girl went and got the baby's mother.

Exodus 2:4–8

During a tragic period in Israel's history, a time of slavery and infanticide, a mother rescued her son from certain death. To do so, she risked hiding him in a basket among the reeds in the river.

Moses' sister watched the basket and perceived an opportunity to save his life when the daughter of Pharaoh found him. She also perceived a need she could meet and brought Moses' own mother to nurse him. Ironically, Moses was entrusted to the custody of his enemy! Moses' family had the presence of mind not only to remove their baby from imminent danger, but also to watch and wait and take further action for his welfare. Then they trusted God for the rest.

121

How difficult it is during a personal crisis to think calmly and clearly and to place focus on those who are most at risk. Our children of divorce are at risk. Parents can come to the rescue simply by being perceptive.

Stop. During the aftermath of divorce, it takes a deliberate effort to stop focusing on self and start focusing on the children. Wallerstein states:

> One of the many myths of our culture is that divorce automatically rescues children from an unhappy marriage. . . . However, when one looks at the thousands of children that my colleagues and I have interviewed at our center since 1980, most of whom were from moderately unhappy marriages that ended in divorce, one message is clear: the children do not say they are happier. Rather, they say flatly, "The day my parents divorced is the day my childhood ended."[7]

Parents need to stop that gigantic snowball of myths and self-protective emotions and take notice of the realities created by divorce.

Look. Since children (including teenagers) do not possess adult skills to understand their own emotions, much less to find the words to express them, parents must learn to pay close attention to behavior.

When I was about eight years old, I remember becoming very upset over something my parents did. While I can't remember what it was, I remember being so furious that I went to my bedroom and moved as much furniture as an eight-year-old could move in front of my closed bedroom door. I planned to stay there forever and never talk to my parents again.

Eventually my father talked me out and tried to find out why I was so upset. I couldn't explain it, but his effort to understand was important to me. And I was glad he talked me out of my room. It was almost time for dinner!

My mild example cannot compare to the bottled-up emotions some children have, especially concerning the breakup of the family. We prefer to avoid knowing how we may have hurt others, so the behaviors communicating that pain might be ignored. Don't ignore them, but rather watch closely and investigate them.

Symptoms of physical sickness like headaches, stomachaches, and breathing struggles might be related to emotional turmoil. Also, changes in behavior such as lying, stealing, violence, or clinginess strongly suggest that children have emotional needs that are not being met.

When new behaviors and strange symptoms emerge, parents can, in an attitude of compassion and empathy, help their children verbalize what is going on inside. If words do not work, encourage children to draw a picture that represents how they are feeling or why they are feeling it.

Listen. Then listen to the response, uncritically, unemotionally, and courageously. Children, like all of us, cannot help the feelings they have. Sometimes lies creep into children's hearts and minds, and they merely need to be corrected. Kids often believe they caused the breakup, or they may fear that the custodial parent will abandon them. Many children feel they have to choose between their parents. Knowing what goes on in a child's mind is over half the battle.

Listen also to anything said within your hearing. Many older children fear direct confrontation and try to communicate their opinions or concerns indirectly. The fake and exaggerated clearing-of-the-throat when your child wants you to hear or notice something should not go ignored. Comments about issues or television programs also might be covert ways to send a parent a message. It is easy to become defensive and reject the way a message was sent, but rejection will make a child more reluctant to try the next time. Just listen.

Be Near

But Ruth replied, "Don't urge me to leave you or to turn back from you. Where you go I will go, and where you stay I will stay.

Your people will be my people and your God my God. Where you die I will die, and there I will be buried. May the LORD deal with me, be it ever so severely, if anything but death separates you and me."

Ruth 1:16–17

Ruth had the right idea when it came to family commitment and loyalty. She considered her mother-in-law her only family and promised to always be near her, physically, spiritually, and emotionally.

If we could do it all over, one thing I wish my husband and I had done differently would be to have lived closer to his daughters. We lived only fifty miles apart. But even that small distance put additional stresses on the relationships. Each daddy weekend Carl looked forward to picking up the girls, but three to four hours of sometimes bumper-to-bumper traffic caused driving stresses that decreased the quality of that precious time with them. Fifty miles prohibited spontaneous visits on either our part or their part, as well as our ability to make it to school events and many of their extracurricular activities.

When they became teenagers and their focus turned from family to friends, the visits to our home grew less and less frequent as daddy weekends conflicted with their social lives or weekend jobs. Had we lived nearby, contact would have been easier to maintain, and we all would have experienced more freedom to come and go at will rather than be confined to a court order. Had we been physically near, it would have been easier to be emotionally and spiritually near as well.

Be a Team

Two are better than one,
    because they have a good return for their work:
If one falls down,
    his friend can help him up.

But pity the man who falls
and has no one to help him up! . . .
Though one may be overpowered,
two can defend themselves.
A cord of three strands is not quickly broken.

Ecclesiastes 4:9–12

Team: "two or more draft animals harnessed to the same vehicle or implement."[8]

What an image for coparenting! Two (or more) adults in the same yoke, tied to the same child. If they don't pull together, they can't make much progress. If one sits down, they go nowhere. If one pulls an opposite direction, they go nowhere or must drag the others along.

Yet what it takes for divorced couples to see themselves as a team for the purpose of parenting can be described only as a miracle. The circumstances of a divorce and the events leading up to it effectively place them on opposing sides. No legal mandate can force them to make that paradigm shift; the choice is completely theirs to responsibly partner together for the sake of the kids, or not. As any coach will avow, "Attitude is everything!"

Consider the criteria for good teamwork. First a team needs an agreed-upon goal. Because divorced parents many times have values that don't exactly harmonize, this might be the trickiest part. The goal might be very broad, such as "We will raise our children to know that they are loved by two parents." A team without a common goal cannot begin to play the game.

Second, teams need a game plan. Parents should plan together how to reach the goal. What roles will each parent play? What roles do they want the stepparents to play? What are their individual strengths? What are their weaknesses? How can they help each other? How can they prevent mistakes? How will they ensure that children do not play them against each other? What

125

strategies can be negotiated to facilitate the most desires of each parent for the kids?

Third, with every kind of team, good communication is a must. A football team planning to run a two-point conversion play must tell the field goal kicker. A baseball coach who wants the batter to bunt so that the runner on third base can score needs to fill in the runner on third base. A parent who wants to break a child of the new habit of lying will need to communicate the problem and the strategy to the other parent.

Fourth, each team member must pull his or her weight. As already noted, one team member slacking off can cause the whole team to fail. One way to help pull the weight is to divide parenting tasks when possible. Jobs that typically are covered by the residential parent could in many cases be done by the other parent, such as clothes shopping; taxiing between school, home, and extracurricular activities; library trips; doctor and dentist appointments. The more both parents take part in parenting tasks, the more the child will feel connected to each as a parent.

It would take a real miracle to accomplish all of these things in your coparenting. They are not one-time changes, but day-to-day, incremental decisions. Be encouraged that every effort made will improve the family life of your child. Hopefully your child will be able to express sentiments similar to these from the journal of a ten-year-old boy:

> When my parents were divorced, I was very sad and I thought it was my fault. Each night after the divorce, I said a short prayer, asking God to help me feel better. Soon I felt a whole lot better. My parents treated me the same as always.
>
> Children often worry that one of their parents will have to leave and never see them again. That is not right. Parents will always understand and try to work out an even schedule.[9]

The primary burden for assuring that children receive the quality of postdivorce parenting that they need and deserve falls not upon the courts but upon the parents and their willingness to be healed, to be unified in parenting, and to be "there."

Be healed. Be unified. Be there.

Check Your Vision

1. Recall your last few interactions with your former spouse. Was the tone of your communication mostly healthy? Did you feel a need to win on an issue? Did you send any messages with your child that should have been delivered by you to your ex-spouse?

2. How do you feel when your child talks about your former spouse? Do you feel vindicated when your child is angry with your ex? Do you get irritated when your child speaks highly of your ex?

3. Make two columns on a piece of paper. In one column, describe how you perceive your relationship with your former spouse. In the other column, describe how your relationship should be if you see that person only as a co-parent and nothing else. How do the descriptions differ? Pick one thing to work on toward a better coparenting relationship.

9

Weed Killer #2:
Proactive Stepparenting

From Eggshells to Empathy

D ear God. Just tell me what to do. Nothing I've tried seems to work. Just tell me what to do."

As a stepmother, this was my prayer more than once in the few years my stepdaughter lived with us. Numerous times I changed my approach to her, hoping to find a happy medium from which to base our new relationship—one in which I could be a friend to her, maintain integrity as a responsible guardian, and not overstep boundaries as a "not-the-momma."

Like most stepparents, I desired to have a loving relationship with my stepchildren. It didn't occur to me that a day would come when a stepchild would reject me. I never expected that my husband would be torn between us or that others would come to suspect that I didn't provide her with proper care. I was perceived to be malevolent, and defending myself seemed futile.

Stepparents who act as a gentle influence can be a positive presence in their families. Stepparents who engage stepchildren in the battle for power and control will likely become that dreaded malevolent being. Either way, how others *perceive* the stepparent may be mostly beyond his or her control.

In my research for this chapter, virtually every book or article I read on stepparenting referenced the ill-famed stepmothers of Cinderella, Snow White, and Sleeping Beauty. Rarely do stepparents appear in children's literature as anything other than sinister. Children therefore grow up with images of stepparents as hateful, jealous, and cruel.

Those negative images combine with the lack of blood connection to create tainted filters through which stepkids, biological parents, and sometimes other outsiders view the stepparent. Stepparents can try to position themselves in a better light, but they are powerless to remove those filters from the eyes of those who observe them.

Does that mean stepparents are doomed to an eggshell existence, forever tiptoeing through stepfamily life, trying not to upset the status quo? Definitely not! That eggshell existence is based upon fear, and the Christian stepparent must remember: "God hath not given us the spirit of fear; but of power, and of love, and of a sound mind" (2 Tim. 1:7 KJV). In this chapter, we'll see how to move from walking on eggshells to having an empathetic relationship with your stepkids.

A Spirit of Fear:
The Eggshell Stepparent

Second Timothy 1:7 in the Amplified Bible says, "For God did not give us a spirit of timidity (of cowardice, of craven and cringing and fawning fear)" (AMP). *Strong's Concordance* also includes the word *dread*. If you are a stepparent, you can probably relate to these words, at least from time to time during your experience. Maybe you can relate to Mark in the following story.

Mark married Sally when her two sons, Blake and Jason, were twelve and fourteen years old. They married in May, so the family would have the summer to adjust. Mark and the boys got along fairly well, both before the wedding and also during the summer.

Then the honeymoon ended. They returned from vacation just in time for school to start. Since Sally never had problems getting the boys to bed on school nights, she'd never really set any rules. But Jason, about to enter high school, began to spend lots of time on the phone at night. Mark and Sally discussed it and decided there should be no more phone calls after 10:00, and phone calls should last no more than thirty minutes. Jason glared at Mark and mumbled, "Why all the rules all of a sudden?"

A few days later, Mark caught Blake lighting up a cigarette in the alley by their driveway. Mark had to tell Sally. Sally confronted Blake, and he denied it (even though Mark had the cigarettes to prove it). Sally grounded Blake for two weeks.

Blake, hoping to get a break at his dad's house, told Sally's ex-husband that Mark "stays on our case all the time, and mom believes him over us!" Sally's ex-husband, who had already put them all through a horrendous custody battle, threatened to take it back to court if he heard any more "abuse stories" about Mark. Sally was upset for days after the phone call.

It seemed like Mark always just "happened" to discover the boys acting up, and Sally began to question Mark's motives. "Are you doing this to turn me against my boys?" Mark regretted he'd ever said anything. He decided it might be better if he just backed out of the whole parenting scene. Mark crawled into his shell and avoided the boys as much as possible.

This fictional example, though based on typical stepfamily dynamics, illustrates one kind of eggshell existence for stepparents: Hear no evil, see no evil, speak no truth. Afraid of rocking the boat, stepparents may abdicate any kind of responsibility for the kids to keep themselves out of the line of fire and maintain peace. While it may be peaceful on the surface, the result is inner turmoil. Not only do they live in a shell, they also feel as if they are walking on eggshells and typecast into that malevolent stepparent role.

Sometimes that stepparent fights to reverse the situation. He or she begins to fulfill the typecast malevolent role by seeking to prevent *all* evil and maintain control to avoid getting burned. Some surefire ways to protect your own false sense of well-being are as follows:

- Make the stepkids feel like outsiders in your home. Don't give them their own things or their own space at your house.
- Monopolize the biological parent's time on visitation weekends.
- Be sure to communicate these sometimes nonverbal messages often:

"You're in my house, and what I say goes."
"Your parents aren't raising you right."
"My own kids are angels compared to you."
"It doesn't matter what you think or feel."
"I'd rather prove I'm 'right' than build a relationship with you."

Obviously, these are very destructive suggestions meant to prove a point. When we act out of fear, there are no positive outcomes. No one learns what true relationships are about, no one really belongs, and no one matures to become trusting, loving, respectful, or at ease. The whole family is on edge, and often at risk.

Conversely, stepparents who walk by faith rather than by sight, who learn to see their stepfamily through the eyes of the kids, and who base their actions on what can be rather than on what is, will contribute to an atmosphere of acceptance and belonging in the stepfamily home. Rather than reacting with harmful defensive strategies (such as those previously noted), empathetic stepparents will more often communicate messages like the following:

- "You are a valued member of this family."
- "I know life seems unfair at times, but I promise to be a responsible and dependable person for you."
- "Your feelings matter to me."

A Spirit of Power: The Informed and Disciplined Step

Two years after Chris's first wife passed away, he met and married Dana. Chris looked forward to Dana's presence in the home to be that nurturing mother influence for his kids. Chloe was seven and Mandy was ten.

Mandy was accustomed to being the woman of the house. She did the laundry, kept the kitchen clean, and even made a grocery list for her dad each Saturday so she could make lunches for Chloe and her to take to school. Dana sensed that Mandy felt threatened by her and that their relationship could be a big challenge.

Although Dana wanted to set up her own system of housekeeping, she realized that Mandy took pride in her chores. To move in and change everything would create resentment in Mandy. Dana recalled how her own stepmom had moved in one day and totally redecorated their rooms. She still had to work on

133

forgiving her stepmom for that—a breach she hoped never to have between herself and the girls.

While they lived in the apartment, Dana left everything just as Mandy had it. When they moved into a new home, Dana solicited Mandy's help setting up the kitchen. Mandy helped willingly but resisted attaching to Dana.

For the first year, Mandy complained about everything Dana did—the oatmeal was different from her dad's, the meatloaf had too much sauce, the towels were folded wrong. Mandy wanted her old room back, she hated her new school, and most of all she wished her mother was still alive. Dana and Chris took every opportunity to assure Mandy of their love and commitment, but Dana did not push for a relationship with her. Her heart broke for Mandy's pain, but she often wondered if things would ever get better between them.

Over the second year, Mandy began to notice how fun Dana was to be with, how she really seemed to enjoy making the costume for her school play, and how Dana cheered for her at her ball games. Dana's heart burst with joy the day Mandy said to her coach, "Coach, this is my mom."

Power Point 1: Knowledge Is Power

"Getting" stepfamily life is empowering—like having the right tools and knowing how to use them. Step relationships cannot work the same as biological relationships, so expecting that is like cutting against the grain of a hard wood; it creates splinters and rough edges. A stepparent will benefit from a careful study of the texture, so to speak, of his or her unique situation. By working with the grain instead of against it, he or she can more gently carve a proper fit into the family, rather than hacking a way in, only to damage the integrity of the whole.

Many factors combine to form a unique framework within which a stepparent must work:

- The stepparent's gender
- The stepchildren's genders and ages
- Whether or not the stepparent is the custodial stepparent or the visitation stepparent
- The relationship quality between the children and their biological parents
- The stepparent's history
- Whether or not the stepparent has his or her own children
- The adjustments the stepchildren have to make, such as:
  Adjusting to the breakup of their parents
  Moving to a new home
  Changing schools
  Getting used to new stepsiblings and half-siblings
  Sharing a bedroom
  Being shuffled between homes
- Any other element of stepfamily life that differs from a child's previous routine

Because of these variables, each stepparent will make his or her own distinct journey. But thanks to stepfamily research, some generalizations can be made about the major stepparent-stepchild combinations, which can be used to guide stepparents in their relationship-building efforts.

STEPMOTHER FAMILIES

Women are relational, emotional creatures by design. The desires to love, nurture, and closely relate to family members are all good. These longings, however, may work to a stepmom's disadvantage when trying to win the hearts of her stepkids. Research has shown that, just as Cinderella and Snow White would have us believe, indeed stepmother-stepchild relationships are more treacherous than stepfather-stepchild relationships.[1] Newton's second law of motion kicks in when a stepmom pushes for relationship: "For every action, there is an equal *and opposite* reaction."

Beth and Gordon had been married for ten months. Gordon had a son, Brandon, who was eight, and a daughter, Kelly, who was ten. Kelly and Brandon liked Beth at first. She seemed nice, she was pretty, and she always had their favorite treats on hand.

Beth hoped to become their second mother. She also wanted to show Gordon how committed she was to the family and to making them feel included. So she began doing all the things a mom would do.

One daddy weekend, Beth passed Kelly's bedroom just as Kelly said, "Can you believe this stupid dress she bought me? How old does she think I am? Three?"

"Yeah, I know. I hate coming over here. It's like she thinks she's our mom or something," said Brandon.

Beth tried some different approaches, but each attempt seemed only to create more resistance. Finally, her feelings were so crushed that she shifted her relationship efforts to Gordon. She wasn't feeling like a part of the family and needed Gordon's affirmation to convince her otherwise. If the kids weren't going to accept her, it was pointless to try anyway.

Kelly and Brandon noticed Beth's attitude change. They reasoned that Beth was trying to get back at them. She made herself look "so good and perfect" to their father and made them look "like brats!" Well, they could make her look bad too! So they withdrew from her even further and competed to win back their dad's love.

Beth's hypothetical experience mirrors that of many stepmoms—a desire to succeed turns into a downward spiral of deeper and deeper resentments and miscommunications. Women try hardest to win the affections of stepchildren. But children expect stepparents to remain distant—especially if their biological parents remain reasonably involved in their lives.[2] The stepmom's relationship pursuits often create splintering rather than bonding.

The visitation stepmom, as in Beth's situation, is the most common stepmother setting. The visitation stepmom has the added disadvantage of being the most "outside" of all the step relationships. She does not live with the kids, nor does she have a biological bond.

If she has her own children as well, bonding is an even greater challenge. Stepkids cannot compete with the bond she already shares with her biological children, making it difficult for her to appear fair and impartial. Also, the household routines she hopes to maintain on visitation weekends may rob the stepkids of treasured playtime with Daddy that they enjoyed prior to the marriage. Fathers who want to work toward a stable stepfamily life will realize that structure (balancing fun with responsibilities) makes for a healthier environment, and they will lead the way to make that adjustment in the new stepfamily.

To establish a healthy balance of fun and responsibility a couple can:

- Discuss how they each envision the family responsibilities to be divided
- Negotiate a plan. The plan should:
  Include all family members
  Allow for free time, family time, and one-on-one time with biological parents
  Fairly distribute tasks according to the abilities of each family member
  Be flexible and creative to allow children to remain involved in usual extracurricular activities, yet make sure they have responsibility for something while in your home

137

The plan should *not* place an undue burden on visitation children. For example, do not dump all the regular chores of the residential children on the visitation children during their visits. If residential children take care of dinner dishes, divide the kitchen duties equally between all children present in the home during visitation weekends.

Nonresident children have a deep need to know that they are as valued and needed by the family as the resident children. They will also be hypersensitive to favoritism and unfairness. Adhering to a structure that emphasizes equality, cooperation, and fun is one way to counter some typical stepfamily curses.

The residential stepmom home occurs in cases of widowhood of the husband, in cases of joint physical custody, or when the father has been granted primary custody. If the stepmother has no children of her own, there is typically an imbalance of authority; the biological father has all of the inherent power if the couple does not recognize that issue and agree to work as a team.[3]

The stepmother-stepdaughter relationship is the most precarious of all step combinations. Stepdaughters are very loyal to their biological parents. Where children of intact homes find security in the strong marital bond of the parents, a stepdaughter sees the parent-stepparent bond as competition to her bond with her parent. A stepdaughter with a strong relationship with her biological mom will not have a need for relationship with a stepmom. So good relationships elsewhere contribute to weak relationships between stepdaughter and stepmother.[4]

Stepsons do not perceive the stepmother-stepson relationship so negatively. Stepsons can accept the additional support offered by stepmothers. Also, the strong marital relationship between father and stepmother typically aids in a stepson's adjustment to stepfamily life.[5]

Unresolved hostility and emotional distance between a father and his children is another challenge for stepmothers. In this situation stepmothers, who want close ties for the whole family, slip into the mode of emotional repairman. They try to fix everything and push the father to put more effort into his relationship with his kids.[6]

It is difficult for a stepmother to establish a quality relationship with a stepchild when the father's relationship remains weak. A father's independent efforts to strengthen ties with his children will help prevent stepmoms from slipping into this controlling "fix-it" mode. Then stepmoms will be free to focus more on their own relationships.

STEPFATHER FAMILIES

Fortunately for stepfathers, their natural lack of emphasis on relationship works fairly well for stepfamilies. Stepkids expect distance from stepparents, and that is what they usually get from stepfathers.

This is not to say that stepfathers remain detached. Rather, because they are not so intent on relationship as stepmothers tend to be, they can have a more natural development of relationship with less pressure on the stepchildren to bond. Even if biological fathers keep in close contact with children, the relationship with the stepfather is not usually adversely affected.[7]

Residential stepfathers (when the custodial mother marries or remarries) make up the majority of stepfather scenarios. One challenge faced by stepfathers is the imbalance of power. The father figure, who typically provides the backbone for discipline and character building in families, will not initially have the authority to do so with his stepchildren. His own children, if any, usually do not live with him. By virtue of her blood ties, the mother has more authority over her children in the home.[8]

Mothers and stepfathers can work together to establish the stepfather's role in the home. As trust is built between stepfathers and stepchildren, the authority can begin to be shared. Here are some ways to transition authority:

139

- The stepfather begins by supporting the mother in her parenting.
- After he builds trust and learns how the family works, the mother might seek his input on parenting matters.
- As the mother implements new policies, the ownership for them might begin to transition from a "my rules" to an "our rules" wording.
- Together, the stepfather and mother solicit input from the children so that they will know their feelings still matter.

The stepfather-stepdaughter relationship is the most difficult one for stepfathers. Once again the daughter's loyalty to her biological parents fights against her need to have a relationship with her stepfather.[9] Also, the difference in gender can make for uncomfortable interaction, especially as the stepdaughter enters puberty and becomes more sexually aware.

Powerful stepparents and their spouses will get to know the territory and understand the possibilities prior to embarking on a relationship strategy. A key source of power is found in allowing God to develop in them the vital fruit of the spirit: self-control.

Power Point 2: Self-Control

In their study guide *Fruits of the Spirit: The Stepfamily Spiritual Journey,* Steve and Dena Sposato apply the fruits of the Spirit in Galatians 5:22–23 to stepfamily life. The first fruit they choose to tackle, I believe with good reason, is that of self-control. They state, "Self-control is not about having strength and willpower—it is the absence of trying to control others."[10]

Self-control means living authentically. We can become too focused on imposing our own values, routines, standards, and beliefs on our stepkids, spouses, or ex-spouses in order to "straighten them out" or "teach them a better way." Interestingly, even Jesus, who was perfect, did not spend his time on earth trying to straighten us out. Instead, he *showed* us the way by living a perfect life, he taught the way when people were hungry to hear, then he sacrificed *his* life to prove how serious he was about ours.

It takes time to learn the territory in stepfamily life. Our natural tendency when we discover those hot buttons is to immediately expose the problem and try to solve it. But while traveling along the learning curve, a stepparent's best defense is a good offense: live an authentic life.

Many times, the people who make the biggest impression on us are not those who tell us how to live, but those who *show* us how to live. Self-control means staying off your soapbox. I fondly remember some good discussions with both of my stepdaughters when they were struggling to determine their own positions on different issues. Those conversation starters just seemed to come from out of the blue: "What's so bad about smoking?" or "I'll never get a divorce. I'll never do that to my kids." Wow! In many of those instances, I was glad to have controlled my words and just answered the questions honestly without malice, fear, or preaching.

Unfortunately, my lack of self-control in other areas contributed to stress in our relationships. When opportunities for discipline arose, I controlled myself enough to have the discussions with my husband without exploding on my stepdaughter. But if the disciplinary action did not meet with my approval, self-control went out the window, and so did our united front. In the front door waltzed "the wicked stepmom" persona, and she never moved out. Self-control sometimes means putting aside your own preferences in order to maintain that powerful solidarity with your spouse.

Self-control means choosing battles wisely. If an issue is not important to both you and your spouse (the biological parent), think twice before bringing it up. If the issue is truly important, first gently win the support of your spouse. Harping and nagging make us stepparents feel better sometimes and may get quick results for the short term, but in the long run we end up being our own worst enemy.

Power Point 3:
Know That God Is in Control

A critical element in moving from that fearful eggshell existence as a stepparent into the realm of being a powerful presence is confidence that God indeed *is* in control. What a burden that takes off of us! We don't have to control everything, and he can work his plan through us in our stepfamilies!

Faith in God guards our hearts against hurtful words or behaviors of stepchildren. We know that if we are faithful to God in our role as stepparent, the rest is up to him.

Through faithful stepparents, Christ brings his presence into our families. Think about stepchildren and all they have been through so far in their lives. Have they seen much of God's love and faithfulness demonstrated in previous role models? We have an opportunity to let God touch them through us. What an awesome and humbling privilege!

We know that God uses suffering to perfect our hearts:

> As iron sharpens iron,
> so one man sharpens another.
>
> Proverbs 27:17

> For you, O God, tested us;
> you refined us like silver.
>
> Psalm 66:10

> Endure hardship as discipline; God is treating you as sons.
>
> Hebrews 12:7

From Genesis through Revelation, men and women demonstrated their reliance on God by following him when it didn't really make sense to do so. They trusted that God had them in a certain place "for such a time as this" (Esther 4:14).

A Spirit of Love: The Empathetic Step

Webster's defines *empathy* as "the action of understanding, being aware of, being sensitive to, and vicariously experiencing the feelings, thoughts, and experience of another."[11] The most helpful tool in changing my own heart toward my stepdaughter was that of learning about the effects of divorce on children. I learned that to expect these kids to always embrace their step-family and behave according to our wishes is simply naive at best and totally unreasonable at worst. Stepchildren work hard to protect themselves from further pain and disappointment. Sometimes they also work to put back the pieces of the intact family they once had. Still others look for destructive ways to express their deep anger and resentment, because they know no other way to get it out. Parents *should* help their kids process those emotions and heal the wounds. Yet parents themselves have difficulty owning the damage their actions caused, and therefore are slow to come to their children's aid.

Returning to the previous example of Beth and her stepkids, Beth began to notice how competitive she had become with the kids for Gordon's attention. She didn't like the resentment she felt toward them, and she knew it was both wrong and wreaking havoc in their family. As she began to try to understand how the kids perceived her and how they felt about their parents' divorce, her heart began to soften toward them. Even when they tried to provoke her into a malevolent response, she remained calm in spite of the hurt she felt in her heart.

Even when the kids began to lie about her to their mom and dad to make Beth appear evil, she welcomed opportunities to do good for them, yet without pushing or forcing her way in. Sometimes it seemed as if things would never change, yet she felt God's peace in her heart and didn't lose hope.

If you were your stepchild, how would you feel? What would you think? What would you want to have happen? As we try to

143

walk a mile in their Nikes, God can help us make connections or keep us from blowing a fuse.

Stepparenting is a life role for which no one ever prepares. There are parenting classes but no stepparenting classes. Our moms and dads train us to be husbands and wives and parents to our own biological children, but they don't try to prepare us for divorce, remarriage, and stepfamily life. If you grew up in a stepfamily, remember, no one trained your stepparents either! It is often a fly-by-the-seat-of-your-pants adventure; thus, the prevalence of self-doubt, insecurity, and fear.

My prayer for stepparents is that those unstable feelings we experience from time to time will always drive us to the one who can help us persevere, who will use us in his redemptive work, and who will replace that fear with power, with soundness of mind, and ultimately with compassion and the perfect love of Christ.

Check Your Vision

1. On the scale below, where would you characterize your current relationship with your stepchildren?

1	2	3	4	5
Walking on eggshells			Walking in empathy	

2. What kind of "spirit" does your presence exude in your stepfamily: malevolence, intercession, enthusiasm, influence, encouragement, loyalty, guidance, comfort, courage, companionship, breath of life, protection?
3. If you are a stepparent, consider some of your protective instincts that automatically kick in and potentially make your situation worse. List them and plan ways to counteract those reactions next time they threaten to occur.

4. Spend some time journaling answers to the following questions to help you move toward having power, love, and soundness of mind regarding your role in the stepfamily:

How has God already used you in your stepfamily? How might he use you in the future?

Write about each of your kids and stepkids. What are their life stories? How have they been hurt along the way?

What issues about your stepfamily really cause your blood to boil? How have you tried to deal with those issues thus far? What has worked? What hasn't, and how could it be done differently?

5. If you are a parent, ask your spouse how well he or she feels supported by you. Are you functioning as a team and making the marriage the backbone of the family? Have an open conversation to discover how each of you perceives the stepfamily situation and what could be improved upon.

10

Weed Killer #3: Constructive Discipline

Making and Maintaining
Family Rules

Discipline. Does any stepfamily issue contain more peril than that of disciplining the kids? Differences in parenting styles, the weaker relationships between stepparents and stepkids, the broken relationship between biological parents, and the fact that the families of origin have established cultures that will clash in many ways—all these elements combine into a volatile mixture that may explode if not handled with care.

Do any of these concerns sound familiar?

- "If you keep rescuing him from his mistakes, he'll never learn how to cope in the real world!"

147

- "She thinks she can just come over here and get waited on hand and foot. I'm not her maid!"
- "When are you going to make them clean up after themselves?"
- "We don't have to do that at Mom's house!"
- "I don't have to mind you—you're not my mom/dad!"
- "Stop being so hard on the kids! You don't understand all they've been through."
- "It's not fair that Jim's kids get away with stuff that we get punished for!"

Nothing is new under the sun. It is a rare occurrence if a stepfamily does not experience many of the above challenges. Often it seems that stepcouples become polarized in their parenting—one heavily standing on the side of truth and discipline and the other on the side of grace and leniency. And kids, being kids, stand strongly on the side of using the division to their own perceived advantage. Rather than remaining at odds in their parenting, couples can combine their styles for a more balanced and unified approach.

What Is Discipline?

"My son, do not make light of the Lord's discipline,
  and do not lose heart when he rebukes you,
because the Lord disciplines those he loves,
  and he punishes everyone he accepts as a son." . . .

Our fathers disciplined us for a little while as they thought best; but God disciplines us for our good, that we may share in his holiness. No discipline seems pleasant at the time, but painful. Later on, however, it produces a harvest of righteousness and peace for those who have been trained by it.

Hebrews 12:5–11

What Discipline Is

The concept of *discipline* is multifaceted according to the dictionary definition. It includes punishment; instruction; training that corrects, molds, or perfects the mental faculties or moral character; control gained by enforcing obedience or order; self-control; and a system of rules that govern conduct or activity.[1] As parents, we hope to favor the more positive aspects—like instilling our kids with high moral character and helping them develop self-control. But often those of us in stepfamilies find ourselves in the roles of enforcers and punishers reacting to violations we never dreamed we would encounter.

As the dictionary definition reveals, discipline is much more than punishment. Training, instruction, and a well-thought-out and well-communicated system of rules should already have been implemented before correction and punishment can be useful or valid. And as the passage from Hebrews reveals, discipline is an act of supreme love and a duty of every parent. It is never pleasant for either the parent or the child but can yield a harvest of righteousness and peace that will be worth the effort in the end.

What Discipline Is Not

Discipline is not a weapon to obtain power. Stepparents often create more problems for themselves when discipline is used as a tool to "put the kids in their place." When it becomes apparent that the kids are not responding with obedience and respect, stepparents may react by tightening the reins to show who is in control. Discipline becomes a means of protecting the parent's place in the home, rather than a means of training, instruction, and correction for the benefit of the child.

In her book *Blended Families*, Maxine Marsolini tells the story of Brent, whose mother remarried when he was eight. When his stepfather moved in, he had to adapt to his stepfather's rules, which were very different from those of his mother. Brent stated,

"My mom always had to check with my stepdad about everything. She thought differently from him on a lot of subjects, but what he said went."[2] He goes on to say he felt like an outsider and had to watch everything he did to stay out of trouble. The stepfather's desire to control his home took precedence over Brent's needs. Discipline became an oppressive tool.

Discipline is not a weapon of vengeance. No matter how many wrongs we suffer in our stepfamily situation, the heart of all discipline should be to provide instruction and correction that will train our kids how to make right life choices. But the insults we suffer make us want to see our kids paid back for the turmoil they cause us—especially if they are not our biological kids.

If we get to the point that we say in our hearts, "This is going to hurt *you* a lot more than it will hurt me (heh, heh, heh!)," then we have a problem. Pride, anger, hate, and our own desires for justice must be placed at the cross of Christ before we can be effective in our parenting roles.

Know Your Discipline Styles

Parents should be aware of the various discipline styles (authoritarian, permissive, and authoritative) and the typical results for the child under each style, so that any style changes will be made for the better, not for the worse.

- *Authoritarian parents* have high, firmly enforced standards with little regard for a child's uniqueness. They fail to provide children with all the support they need to achieve the high standards they set. If a child is well-behaved and order is maintained in the house, then authoritarian parents feel they have done their job. These kids might be well-behaved, but they also are fearful of trying new things and distrustful of others.[3]

- *Permissive parents* accept a child regardless of behavior and set few limits or standards for the child. They do enough to maintain physical safety, but otherwise the child acts mainly upon his or her own discretion. Children parented in this manner are the least competent, least self-controlled, and least mature.[4]

- *Authoritative parents* balance firm control of a child's behavior with allowing the child some independence and encouraging his or her individuality. They maintain high standards while simultaneously providing lots of support and opportunity for successes. Children parented with this style are more likely to be competent, self-confident, and self-controlled.[5]

The authoritative style, which is most effective, is much harder to maintain following divorce and remarriage. Guilt and the lack of two-parent, in-home support may cause residential parents to lean toward a more lenient style. Resentment over loss of control may cause nonresidential parents to tend toward a more authoritarian style when kids are in their home.

Stepparents jockeying for position may also find it difficult to establish an authoritative style. If they want relationship they may become permissive, and if they want control they may become authoritarian. These dilemmas can be best solved as remarried couples refocus on the needs of their kids (rather than their own needs for relationship or control) and unify for the purpose of instructing, training, and providing correction.

Family Rules: Toward Unity in Discipline

I remember playing hide-and-seek with my brother and sisters and the neighborhood kids. I never really liked the game, but I especially hated being "it." When I finally found a kid hiding, I was too slow to catch him on the mad dash to base. But it seemed like any time I actually almost tagged him, he would rush to a nearby tree, swing set, or fence post and call out, "Safe!"

Suddenly the rules had changed. The back door of the house was no longer the base. Whatever the runner was closest to became base. I never had a chance. So I had to be "it" again (and again and again).

With consistent rules, everyone has a fair chance to make progress. Families of origin naturally form roles and rules that become the norm for relating to others in their family.

For example, the father might take on the provider role, and the mother might become the primary caretaker of the home and all the kids. Maybe Mom and Dad equally share the role of disciplinarian and always try to present a united front before the kids. Maybe the kids each have assigned chores, rules about completing homework before playing outside or watching TV, and ways to earn "fun money" by doing extra chores. Kids know the danger they risk if they ask Mom, "What's for dinner?" every night and that Dad won't tolerate friends calling after 10:00 P.M.

Many family rules form to provide structure and confidence for relationships. The family rules, although they are tested, sometimes violated, and occasionally changed, are in place. Everyone understands where the lines are drawn.

When stepfamilies form, two sets of household rules—each important to the family of origin—enter the picture. Expectations of one family may not agree with those of the other family. Each family believes its way to be right. The once-firm foundation that established a fair playing field is demolished. New rules and expectations must be negotiated and solidified.

Rules change abruptly and often seem unfair. New rules need time to evolve into a state of fairness so that they can be accepted. Where once Mom had plenty of time to spend with her own children, she now must find ways to divide herself between more children. Where once everyone ate at the dinner table together, now certain members can eat in front of the television. Where once bedtime was 9:30 P.M., now it is 9:00 P.M. Where once the children each had their own rooms, now they must share. Most unfairly, children who commute between their biological parents must often adjust to two sets of new rules. Nothing can really be counted on.

When my teenage stepdaughter moved into our home, we were not prepared to negotiate the rules in a way that we all could accept. We did not sit down and talk to her about what rules she had been used to in her mother's home. My husband listed a few rules concerning keeping up her grades in school, curfew, and having friends over. One of his rules was that she could have boys in her room as long as she kept the bedroom door open. He hadn't mentioned that one to me, but I kept my mouth shut.

The first time she tested that rule, of course, I was the adult in charge. After her male friend left, I told her that I wasn't comfortable with that rule, and that when her dad wasn't home, I would rather she keep her guy friends out of the bedrooms. Later my husband and I talked it over. He argued that it should be okay if the bedroom door stayed open. Her bedroom was in the farthest corner of our house, so I argued, "I don't want to be the one checking up on them. Do you?" So that rule changed, which caused a new fracture in my relationship with her—something that could probably have been prevented.

Like my family, stepfamilies often don't take the time necessary to iron the wrinkles out of new rules or make them clear to everyone in the house. Even if they do, it is impossible to immediately redefine everything that took years to establish in the family of origin. The rules evolve as issues arise, usually once someone violates someone else's rights in a new way. But the more time and effort invested initially to develop and communicate policies for the family, the better.

Step One: Make a Plan

To make an initial plan, couples will first need to honestly discuss their hopes and expectations for how the family will function. Some questions you may want to answer are:

- What is your current parenting style?
- What rules are the kids already accustomed to?
- What are the needs of each child in the family?
- What are our desires for our kids? What should the end product look like?
- How should the family function? What roles should each family member play?
- What kinds of policies do we need to work toward the desired outcome (i.e., policies regarding respect for each other; respect for each other's things; chores; homework; bedtime; getting permission; consequences for bad choices; uses of shared items like the phone, television, and bathroom; and so on)?

Where differences in expectations exist, those should become negotiating points for the final plan.

One key to successful stepfamily policies and procedures is to implement them slowly. Maybe you have a list of ten policies you hope to establish in your family. Pick out two or three that are the most important, and work on those first. Change is difficult and comes easier in small doses. Too many changes will cause children to become exasperated—something Ephesians 6:4 warns us against. Exasperation is a precursor to rebellion. Children who feel they cannot live up to the standards set for them will give up trying at all.

A second key to successful stepfamily policies and procedures is flexibility. The family policy should be much like our U.S. Constitution, a growing and living document that *serves* each member and the family as a whole, rather than *controlling* each member. The children may also be involved in shaping policies, but the final draft comes from the couple after they have met behind closed doors to hammer it out.

Step Two: Communicate the Plan

Besides communicating the actual plan, several other messages should be expressed to the family as you attempt a new structure. Your children need to know:

- That you recognize their needs and want to meet those needs.
- What kind of people you hope they will become, and how these policies can help them in that process.
- That each adult carries equal authority in the home, not to oppress them, but to care for them. Teach them the concept of stewardship—that each parent has given the other parent authority to act in his/her place. If, in the parent's absence, the stepparent must make a decision regarding a stepchild, it is as if the parent made that decision.
- That as they grow, and their needs change, so may the policies change to accommodate their needs.
- That you know you aren't perfect and sometimes mistakes will be made, but you will do your best to be fair.

For example: "We love each of you, and we want this home to be a place where you each belong and feel welcome and a part. These are the policies we believe will help our family work best. They will help make sure all of us know what to expect. Both your stepparent and I have the authority to enforce these policies. We will try to be fair, but we may make mistakes sometimes. If you feel you've been treated unfairly, we will sit down

155

later together and discuss it. If we agree, we will do our best to rectify our mistake."

As you meet as a family to communicate new expectations and standards, do so in an attitude of grace. Allow children to ask questions and provide them with thoughtful, complete answers. Acknowledge that the new family is a big adjustment. For those who have been in the stepfamily situation for a while and are now trying to regroup, communicate your regrets over the failings of the past. Honesty and humility will help soften the hearts of family members and build goodwill.

Step Three: Follow Through

Know it is *normal* for children to test the marriage relationship and the stepfamily rules. For a while—and maybe a long while—stepfamily members have an "eggshell existence" as each member hopes not to be the one perceived to cause a conflict. It's kind of like living in a house that hasn't been designed or built yet. No walls, no roof, no privacy. Maybe there's a basic sketch ("the plan"), and maybe a little bit of framing is done, but if a family member sees something that he or she doesn't like, why not just tear it down? In a stepfamily, each individual has a choice: Either be a part of the construction team by cooperating with the new rules or be a part of the wrecking crew by refusing to cooperate.

Remember, in the minds of children, their first family was supposed to last, and it didn't. They have probably, by now, lived under three sets of rules that didn't last (the "intact" family rules and two sets of single-parent rules). Why should this new family arrangement be any different? Some children of divorce have already learned from previous role models that if you don't like the way things are going, just change it, even if someone gets hurt. The task of the remarried couple is to "unlearn" them of that belief and teach them a better way—interdependence, commitment to each other, and responsibility for each other.

These times of testing the rules are trials by fire—the true substance of the remarried couple's relationship will surface. Couples must be prepared to back each other up—at least in front of the kids. Couples must also maintain a mind-set of fairness and avoid temptations to be more lenient with biological kids than with stepkids. In his book *The Smart Stepfamily*, Ron Deal states:

> When changes do occur, children will likely complain, especially if the rules are getting tighter. "You never made us do chores before you married him. He's just bossing you around." Kids are great with manipulation! At a time of change, parents and stepparents must stand together. If there are any chinks in your armor, children will divide and conquer (they think that is their mission in life).[6]

Expect to have many times of testing, persevere calmly through them all, and come out on the other side as the genuine article—the one whose house is "built upon the rock"!

Some Common Discipline Issues

How do we handle the differences in discipline styles between homes?

One common complaint of children is that one home has stricter rules than the other home. This is tricky, because many answers you give can be understood as a criticism against the policies of the other home. Children quickly learn when their parents or stepparents disapprove of the other home's style and can use that knowledge as a divisive weapon.

When confronted with this issue, Ron Deal recommends that parents avoid attacking the other home by using the word *and* rather than the word *but*. For example, "I understand that bedtime at your other house is 9:30, *and* at our house bedtime is 9:00." By using the word *and* instead of *but,* the critical tone doesn't creep in to plant a divisive seed.[7]

Acknowledge the fact that there are differences between your homes. Acknowledge that no two parents will parent the same way, but that parents do their best for their kids. The rules you decided on as a couple are the ones you feel work best for everyone in your stepfamily.

How do I handle a stepchild who defies my authority?

In times like these, we wish God would not have granted our kids a free will, but he did. One answer to this question is, "You don't." Let your spouse, the biological parent, handle your stepchild's issues with authority. The biological parent is the only person who can make a real difference. If your spouse supports and affirms you as an authority figure in your stepchild's life, treats disobedience to you the same as disobedience to him or her, and allows the agreed-upon consequences to take place, the stepchild can learn to respect you as an adult authority.

A spouse who allows the child to escape consequences or to disrespect the stepparent invites turmoil into the home. The stepparent will feel betrayed, and the stepchild can use this power over the stepparent for destructive purposes, weakening both the marriage and the family. Stepchildren may or may not come to appreciate or accept stepparents as parents, but they can learn to respect their authority as they would a schoolteacher or a babysitter. The authority must be conferred to the stepparent and backed up by the parent, or it is not authority at all.

Meanwhile the stepparent can help the situation by trying to understand the cause of a stepchild's defiance. Four possible causes of misbehavior in children are a need for attention, a perceived threat and a need to gain control, retaliation for a hurt that has been done to them, or withdrawal from a situation that makes them feel inadequate.[8] Try to determine the root cause and take steps to meet that need while still maintaining the agreed-upon policies.

My teenage stepson won't clean his room. Should we make him keep it clean?

The answer to that question may apply to many "should we make them do this or that" issues. I believe we must choose our battles based on the whole picture. What are all of the issues you currently deal with, and how does a "clean room"—or whatever—compare to the other issues? How old is the stepchild, and how teachable is he or she? Is the child accustomed to keeping a messy room, or is it a defiant act that is a symptom of a more serious emotional problem? Does the same requirement apply to everyone in the home? Is it just messy, or would the Department of Health quarantine the room because of bacteria cultures growing under the bed and sticky drink spills attracting ants and roaches?

I chose not to make an issue over messy bedrooms. Whenever it was important that the bedroom be cleaned—when company was coming—I notified my stepdaughter, and she willingly got the job done. I also believe that children in stepfamilies have so little control over events in their lives, the bedroom is one area of control they can be granted (within reason, of course) with few negative repercussions. I am still grateful that we avoided at least a few battles over things that were not worth the fight they would have caused.

Discipline in stepfamilies is not as cut-and-dried as it can be in intact homes. So much has already transpired to develop behaviors, attitudes, and emotions that hinder the process of training, instruction, and correction. The best advice I received

159

as a stepmom was "Do what you believe in your heart is right, and trust God for the rest." We cannot control the choices our children and stepchildren will make, but we can be sure we've attempted to train them up in the way they should go, which is all God asks of us.

Check Your Vision

1. What rules changed when your stepfamily formed? How were the new rules communicated? How were they received? How can your family work together to best develop rules and modify them when needed?

2. Out of the three discipline styles (authoritarian, permissive, and authoritative), which describes you best? Which describes your spouse best? If your styles were combined, would your parenting be better or worse?

3. Make a list of the specific discipline issues with which you are currently dealing. Keep in mind that the goal of discipline is training, instruction, and correction (not oppression or revenge), and rank these issues in order of importance.

4. Think about the top three items on your list. Are you and your spouse currently unified in your plan to resolve them? If not, meet on those issues and negotiate a plan.

11

Emotional Fortification for Kids

C hildren face many stresses growing up, but two of their top five stressors are related to their parents. The number one stressor for children is the loss of a parent. The fifth highest stressor is parents who fight. Going blind, flunking a grade in school, and wetting their pants are only slightly worse than having parents who fight.[1]

Unquestionably, the involvement of parents (not only the biological ones, but anyone who "brings up and cares for another") matters to the healthy emotional and social development of children. But if parents' emotional antennae do not remain extended to their children, they risk malnutrition at best and starvation at worst in the emotional and spiritual diets of their kids.

What Kids Need

More than thirty years ago, a question raised at a parenting class on nutrition caused a man named Edward Linzer (later to become the education director of the National Association for Mental Health) to develop a guide for parents called *What Every Child Needs for Good Mental Health*. The question that prompted his interest was, "What do you feed a child's mind and soul?"[2]

How often, as parents, do we consider whether or not we are properly nourishing the minds and souls of our children—providing them with healthy emotional and spiritual nutrients? The eight needs that Linzer found to be necessary "spiritual nutrients" are love, acceptance, security, protection, independence, faith, guidance, and control.[3]

The first four spiritual nutrients—love, acceptance, security, and protection—become difficult to provide following divorce and more difficult following remarriage. Their opposites—fear, rejection, instability, and pain—are unavoidable by-products of stepfamily life.

The last three nutrients (faith, guidance, and control) are sorely lacking in many families. They are especially difficult to work on in stepfamilies due to the differences in beliefs and discipline methods between households and the lack of continuous two-parent involvement.

Independence, the fifth on Linzer's list of emotional needs of children, is conversely too readily available to many children of divorce. They may receive an "overdose" of independence as parents spend more time outside the home, supporting the family or developing their personal lives. Children must fend for themselves without parental guidance in more areas of their lives (i.e., latchkey kids). Through it all, a child's sense of belonging to a family can become progressively weaker. Also, changes in discipline styles after divorce and through remarriage contribute to deficiencies in a child's emotional diet.

The sections to follow describe some emotional developmental tasks of childhood broken down into three major stages: birth to preschool, elementary to preteen, and adolescence. In each stage, two case studies compare the experiences of children from intact homes to the experiences of those from broken and step-family homes. Whatever the ages or stages of your children or stepchildren, try to imagine what emotional supplements they might need.

Emotional Diets from Birth through Preschool

Claire

Claire started kindergarten this year. From the day Claire was born, she has experienced the love and care of both her mom and dad. They were both present when Claire said her first words, took her first steps, and used the potty chair for the first time. When she cried, sometimes her dad comforted her and sometimes her mom did.

Claire's parents argue occasionally, which upsets her, but they always work it out. Claire's parents work together to help her learn to share with others, to not be afraid, to ask for things she wants rather than throwing tantrums, and to protect her from experiences and situations that are not appropriate for a child in her stage of development.

Andrew

Andrew also started kindergarten this year. Andrew's parents divorced when he was three. The first year of his life he experienced lots of love and care from both his parents. Then they began to fight a lot. His mother would always place him in his bed and close the door, but he could still hear them yelling. He became agitated and cried a lot during this time. Andrew's parents went through a time of separation, and sometimes Andrew wouldn't see his dad for several days. When they finally divorced, Andrew had to go somewhere else to see his dad.

163

Now Andrew has a stepmother and two stepsisters. They treat him okay, except for the older sister, who calls him a pest. But Andrew misses his mom when he is at his dad's house. And everything is so different. He sees lots of television that his mom won't let him watch, and they make him go to bed earlier than his mom does. Andrew's mom doesn't like his new stepmother. When his dad picks him up at their house, they usually fight about her. Sometimes Andrew wonders who will pick him up from kindergarten, and he worries that they will forget whose day it is. Maybe no one will pick him up.

Supplementing the Diet for Infants and Preschoolers

Attachment to parents is a major task in this stage of a child's emotional and social development. The life changes brought on by divorce often damage attachment, which then negatively affects subsequent parenting tasks through the teen years.

Work to reinforce attachment by:

- Taking steps to heal your own damaged emotions
- Not undermining attachment with the other parent
- Sticking to similar structures and schedules in both homes
- Continuing to meet both physical and emotional needs to the same degree and in the same way as prior to divorce as much as possible

In addition to the attachment tasks of parents in earliest years, all preschoolers also need a balance of acceptance and behavior control. Preschoolers need to know that their emotions are normal, but they also need to learn what to do with them. Preschoolers need to be encouraged to explore and develop motor and thinking skills. But they also need boundaries and structure to help them feel safe exploring.

The table at the end of this chapter outlines some emotional needs of early childhood, the limitations placed on meeting those needs when couples break up, and some suggestions for making the best effort on behalf of a young child in a stepfamily.

Vitamin C for Infant and Preschool Stepchildren

Some preschoolers seem to adapt well to stepfamily life, but this does not mean they are "over" the emotional stresses caused by divorce and remarriage. Preschoolers suffering hurtful memories of the marriage breakup may resist forming new attachments. They may behave in ways that hurt a stepparent's feelings or cause embarrassment. One common behavior is that of physically trying to separate the parent from the stepparent—sitting between them on the couch, crawling into the middle of a hug, redirecting a parent's face from you to them, and other such behaviors.

When these kinds of things occur, stepparents should bear in mind that they do not indicate failure. This is one way preschoolers express their anger and insecurity over the situation. Rather than taking the rejection personally, try seeing through the child's eyes. Demonstrating patience and compassion will prevent you from leaving that child with an antagonistic memory that might otherwise return to haunt you.

An emotional vitamin that stepparents can offer their toddler or preschool-aged stepchildren is a healthy dose of vitamin C: Be *charitable*.

C *Care* for their physical needs.

H *Help* your spouse nurture emotional attachment to biological children.

165

A Be *available* to be your stepchild's friend.

R Have *reasonable expectations* about your preschool step-child's behavior.

I *Imitate* Christ's compassion for the brokenhearted.

T *Take conflict* behind closed doors, out of a child's earshot, to deal with it.

A Show *affection* to the degree a stepchild can receive it.

B *Bless* your stepchildren with *sincere* praise.

L Be *loyal* to the stepfamily as a whole.

E *Encourage* honesty about feelings. When they act out to get attention, help them discover what really is bothering them.

Nurturing younger stepchildren in these ways, whether you are facing challenges right now or not, will help them strengthen their image of you and their place in the stepfamily. As children reach new levels of maturity, they will likely reevaluate their family life and their relationship with you. The more trust you build now, the better chance of maintaining a good relationship as they grow older.

Emotional Diets during the Elementary Years

Jason

Jason is about to enter middle school. Already he has experienced peer pressure to try smoking and drinking. His parents have always encouraged him to talk to them about anything, so one evening at dinner he told his parents about his best friend who was sneaking alcohol. They helped him understand the temptation he was facing and helped him come up with a plan to handle it.

166

Jason's parents encourage him when he wants to try new skills. His dad helps him in batting practice and guides him in projects for school. His mom doesn't let him off the hook when he doesn't feel like practicing piano. If Jason wants to buy something new, he has to save his allowance so that he can learn the value of work and money. They always expect him to do his best. When Jason is faced with a difficult choice, they help him figure out what might happen either way and give him the opportunity to make the right choice. Sometimes Jason has to suffer consequences of wrong choices, but usually his parents are proud of him for the choices he makes.

Ashley

Eleven-year-old Ashley lives in two stepfamilies. She lives with her mom during the school year and goes to her dad's during holidays and for two months in the summer (he lives in another state). Ashley has a lot of anger toward her mom, who kicked her dad out of the house when Ashley was seven. Her mom married Bill when Ashley was nine, and they moved into his big, expensive house. It was cool that she no longer had to share a room with her little sister, but when Bill's kids come every other weekend, her stepsister sleeps in her room, and they don't get along.

Ashley has learned that whenever she wants new clothes or a new CD, she can get it by making her mom feel guilty for divorcing her dad. Bill expects Ashley's mom to do a lot of entertaining, so the kids spend a lot of time in their rooms when company comes. They don't ever ask Ashley about school or friends. Ashley knows her mom would be shocked if she knew some of the friends she had made.

When she is at her dad's house, she feels like an outsider. She doesn't have her own room or anything that belongs to her. They go to church a lot, and Ashley isn't comfortable around the church kids, so she's never made any friends there. She loves being with her dad, but he tries to keep things so "happy" for them all the time. She can't really talk to him about things that are bothering her because she's afraid of ruining the time for him. The only people she's really comfortable talking to about her problems are her friends at home.

Supplementing the Emotional Diet for Elementary and Preteen Children

Developing self-worth, self-confidence, and self-regulation are the major emotional developmental needs of preadolescent children. To assist children through this stage, even closer attention must be paid to the emotional, social, and moral gauges of elementary children. Unfortunately, the tendency of parents (especially divorced parents) is to withdraw emotionally as children grow older and become more independent.

Parents can reinforce these areas by:

- Providing consistent standards, boundaries, and controls that will challenge them without discouraging them
- Providing lots of support and guidance to help them succeed
- Modeling self-worth, self-confidence, and self-regulation
- Backing up words with deeds—live an authentic life before them
- Spending time letting them talk about what they think and feel
- Valuing their opinions
- Not allowing guilt to affect parenting

The table at the end of this chapter lists some emotional needs of elementary and preteen children, some aspects of divorce that interfere with meeting their needs, and some suggestions for parents to put forth their best effort in bringing children through those years.

Vitamin A for Elementary and Preteen Stepchildren

From ages five to twelve a child's perceptions of a stepparent and his or her stepfamily may change many times. Stepparents may find that this is the most opportune stage of development for being a friend and influencing a child's values and beliefs. Preteen children are curious, can understand some deeper issues, and have not yet become closed-minded to adult perspectives (or stepparent perspectives).

Stepparents can keep supplying doses of vitamin C (be *charitable*) and add to it a dose of vitamin A: Be *approachable*.

A Be *available* to listen and to share your perspective.

P Be *perceptive* of a stepchild's needs and mood changes.

P *Provide* a nurturing environment, including meals and routines that help stepchildren know they matter.

R *Respect* stepchildren the same way you want to be respected.

O *Overlook* their insignificant flaws and annoyances.

A *Avoid defensiveness* when responding to inflammatory situations.

C *Communicate* and honor family rules for politeness and respect.

H *Help* with homework, relationships, and skills they are learning whenever possible, as welcomed by the stepchild to do so.

A *Attend* school activities to show interest and support whenever you are welcomed to do so.

B *Be self-regulated and self-confident,* and know your *self-worth.*

L *Learn* their *love languages.* (What makes your stepchildren feel like they belong?)

E *Encourage* your spouse to connect emotionally with his or her children.

169

Preteen children are on the verge of some monumental changes in their lives. In the coming years, they will strive for greater and greater independence, and stepparents are likely to be the first to experience the teen's efforts to separate from authority figures. Yet a stepparent who has remained approachable may have a valuable opportunity to serve as a mentor during the treacherous years known as adolescence.

Emotional Diets for Teens

Stephanie

Stephanie is about to graduate from high school and can't wait to get out. She was never a part of the "cool" group and has just a few close friends. She still hasn't been out on many dates, and that has really depressed her a lot. But her mom and dad have always told her how proud they are of her. Since she was little, every night her dad has told her, "I love you. Sweet dreams, hon." Her mom has always listened to her talk about the boys she likes, the struggles she has had with friends, and the dream she has to become a veterinarian someday. And even though she's not that good at science in school, they've never discouraged that dream.

Toby

Toby is a sophomore in high school. He moved in with his dad last year, by his own choice. His stepdad was always on his case about his looks, his grades, and his attitude. He knew his stepdad was glad he was out of the house, and his mom was probably relieved to get rid of the tension as well.

Toby's dad was glad he was there, but Toby could tell his dad didn't approve of his looks any more than his stepdad did. Toby's appearance made his dad fear that Toby would get into trouble outside the home, so he set very strict curfews and rules about

170

where Toby could and couldn't go. His stepmom was pretty nice. She tried to make sure Toby felt like he was a part of the family. If Toby and his dad had a fight, she tried to make peace between them. Toby wanted his dad to know him and accept him, but he felt like he was such a disappointment—he would never be the brilliant, athletic son his father wanted.

Supplementing the Emotional Diet of Teens

"Who am I?" "How do others see me?" "How do I *want* others to see me?" "What do I want?" "How do I want to be?" The needs for acceptance, support, and skills in decision making in the search for identity are the overwhelming task of adolescence. Thus, adolescence is a time of continual experimentation with appearance, attitudes, values, beliefs, and behaviors, and of seeking approval among peers. As a reassurance to parents, Ruth Arent states:

> Most adolescents search for self-awareness twenty-four hours a day. They want to face their own problems. They want help only when they ask for it.
> Adolescents are still kids, though commonly cheated of childhood. They are bombarded by confused values and the raw material of relationships and human weaknesses that were not splattered in front of teenagers twenty or twenty-five years ago. They are not protected from painful situations and issues that were sanctified and kept away from kids. They act out in order to discover who they are and what works and doesn't work in society. They do not act out to hurt you.[4]

Teens whose parents are divorced face a greater dilemma in feeling accepted and discovering their identity. First of all, the family they once felt they belonged to no longer exists. Second, the input they receive from divorced parents may conflict and create more confusion. Third, anger and hormones fog a teen's perception of possibilities for his or her life.

171

Divorced parents can work to combat these teen emotional deficiencies by:

- Setting and maintaining boundaries throughout the child's life
- Embodying the character traits they hope to develop in their children
- Listening well without giving advice or judging
- Accepting the children no matter what and supporting them in their process of becoming

The table at the end of this chapter provides a summary of the developmental needs of teenagers, the ways that divorce interferes with meeting them, and some general suggestions for making the best effort to get teens of divorce through the volatility of adolescence.

Vitamin F for Teenage Stepchildren

Stepparenting a teen can be one of the most traumatic experiences of stepfamily life. Adolescence and stepfamilies are an explosive combination. At a time when it is hardest to be that anchor of love, firm guidance, and emotional support, those are the very things that all teens (and to a greater degree, teens of divorce) most need a parent to be.[5]

Teens are in the process of taking control of their lives. Stepparents may feel threatened by a teen's increasing efforts to take charge. Lack of parental bonding causes us to perceive them as spoilers of our own preferred lifestyle and peaceful existence, rather than as developing human beings becoming independent.

Stepparents have a choice. Interpret the radical behaviors of adolescent stepkids as personal attacks and contribute to the atmosphere of conflict in the home by taking defensive measures, or interpret their behaviors as emotional struggles through which most teens must progress and commit to be a stable influence during their time of greatest volatility. (And, yes, the volatility of a teen in a stepfamily will usually be greater than that of a teen in an intact family—so don't be surprised.)

In addition to those healthy doses of vitamins C and A (be *charitable* and *approachable*), offer your teenage stepchildren some of your best vitamin F: Be *flexible*.

F   Be *fun*. Refuse to take everything seriously. Laugh with your stepchild.

L   *Loosen up*. Allow teens to break out of your mold and decide on their own methods and timing for taking care of their responsibilities.

E   *Encourage* them to talk about themselves and their opinions (without fear of being corrected by you).

X   *Expect* them to test everything: authority, your marriage, your values, their boundaries, themselves.

I   *Impress* them with your ability to pass their tests with confidence and tranquility; don't break under the pressure.

B   *Be brave* and try things their way once in a while!

L   *Like them*. Rather than criticizing their faults, verbalize the things you enjoy and appreciate about your stepkids.

E   *Embody* the qualities you hope they will have—such as love, integrity, faith, and contentment.

Finally, pray for your stepkids. Our God is in the business of making good come out of evil. Prayer is part of God's divine plan for working out his redemptive tasks. At the very least, God will, through your prayers, change your own heart toward your stepkids.

Even stepparents who manage to do most of the right things for their family may experience a stepchild who just cannot or will not allow a stepparent into his or her life. Emily and John Visher, founders of the Stepfamily Association of America, offer this comfort to those estranged from their stepkids: "Most adolescents return for an adult-adult relationship when they feel they have discovered what they want for themselves and are ready to relate on an independent basis."[6]

Children of divorce and in stepfamilies are often deprived of emotional nourishment unless parents beef up their diet. Through the preschool years, emotional attachment to parents is the imperative task. If that was accomplished, it will typically make the tasks of the elementary years—those of developing self-confidence, self-worth, and self-regulation—progress with greater ease. And if parents are successful through the elementary years, the trials of adolescence—the "Who am I?" years—might progress with greater ease.

But the stepfamily, by nature, comes with a greater degree of trial and tribulation. When it becomes impossible, think on this passage found in James 1:2–4 (emphasis added):

> Consider it pure joy, my brothers, whenever you face trials of many kinds, because you know that the testing of your faith develops perseverance. *Perseverance must finish its work so that you may be mature and complete, not lacking anything.*

Interestingly, when a Christian parent (or stepparent) keeps on parenting so that his or her kids can become mature and complete, God can use those very trials to mature and complete the parent as well. I wonder if James had parenting in mind as one of those "trials of many kinds." Whether he did or not, just remember to consider it pure joy (and this too shall pass)![7]

Ages and Stages	Some Normal Emotional and Social Needs	Possible Deficiencies Due to Divorce	Additional Needs Created by Divorce and Remarriage	Ingredients for a Healthier Emotional Diet
Infants and toddlers 0–3	**Attachment to Parents:** Physical presence. Positive interactions. Physical needs to be met in a timely and nurturing manner. Affection from parents. Protection of parents. **Encouragement to Explore:** Parents to set limits and provide safety. Attentiveness to toddler's activity. Praise for progress made.	Less access to one or both parents. Toddlers sense tension between former spouses. Unresolved anger vented on child. Each parent adopts a different schedule and procedure for meeting the child's needs, which creates insecurities. Wounds of divorce may cause parents to withhold affection from child. Parents less attentive to child's needs to explore. Parents don't communicate child's progress to each other.	To deal with the strong and deep wounds of divorce that small children suffer but cannot express. To not be exposed to hostilities between parents. To adjust to new routines and relationships. To reestablish trust and security.	Make frequent quality time with child a priority. Be physically available and emotionally responsive. Keep tense interactions between adults behind closed doors and out of the child's hearing. Be healed of your own emotional scars. Communicate with the other parent regarding schedule, likes and dislikes, progress and challenges. As much as possible, match parenting styles and routines between homes. Make changes slowly.

Preschoolers
 	
3–5
	Attachment to Parents:
	Maintain attachment to parents.
	To be accepted by parents.
	
	Guidance and Instruction:
	To learn to control behavior.
	To learn to handle emotions.
		Less access to one or both parents.
		Preschoolers tend to fantasize about reasons for the divorce:
		  Parent no longer loves them.
		  "I'm bad."
		Parents vent frustrations on children.
		Parents avoid dealing with emotions, both their own and those of the children.
		Parents relax parenting efforts out of either guilt or emotional exhaustion.
			To know they did not cause the divorce.
			To know both parents still love them.
			To have consistent routines and parenting styles in both homes.
			To be encouraged by both parents to love the other parent—to not be used in an emotional tug-of-war between households.
			To not be used as a "messenger" between former spouses.
			To adjust to new places, routines, and relationships.
				Divide parenting duties as much as possible. Continue high priority parenting.
				Assure preschoolers of your love frequently. Dispel fantasies that state otherwise.
				Don't speak negatively about the former spouse to your child.
				Both households cooperate on setting and reaching parenting goals for the child.
				Create opportunities for preschoolers to express emotions: reading together and discussing the feelings of the characters, drawing together, etc.

Elementary and Preteen 5–12	To develop self-confidence. To develop self-worth. To develop self-discipline. To develop a healthy outlook. To learn to express feelings. To learn to handle conflict.	Parents often too focused on selves to notice child's achievements. Wounded parents often cannot effectively model self-confidence or self-worth. Children become latch-key kids and are given too much freedom too early in their lives. Learn that conflict is a precursor to ending relationship. Parent may not model or enforce self-restraint or good conflict resolution skills. Feelings of guilt initiate switch to leniency in parenting.	To have as normal a childhood as possible. To not become a care-giver of hurting parents. To not become a confidante of adult concerns. To develop friendships and be able to participate in as many normal childhood activities as possible. To learn the ingredients of healthy relationships. To not be able to play one parent against the other.	Be attentive to child's interests, explorations, and achievements. Be available to answer questions and to guide children. Help children explore their emotions. Deal honestly with feelings. Teach children what good relationships look like, and what bad relationships look like. Maintain an involved, authoritative parenting style, paying close attention to behavior. Maintain communication and a unified front with the other parent.
Adolescence 11–18	To develop their identity. To have increasing independence and a "safe house" for testing it. To understand the changes of puberty. To be accepted by others. To take part in decision making. Support (financial and otherwise). Help in handling their raging hormones and emotions. Consistency in rules and boundaries.	Different expectations from parents frustrate the child—can't make everyone happy. Travel between homes interferes with important relationships with peers. Nonresidential parent often has difficulty adjusting to teen's growing independence. Teens learn to manipulate parents with guilt. If a parent became too lenient in earlier years, he or she will likely be fighting to get the control back during teen years.	Assurance regarding parents' love and reason for the divorce. Stability in their home(s). Honesty about their situation. To have a "normal" teen experience. Hope that they can succeed in future relationships. To learn anger management skills and what to do with feelings of guilt—whether true or false guilt.	Stay attentive to teen and connected to teen (in person and by phone) while providing opportunities to experiment with freedoms. Be a good listener. Stay in close contact with other parent, and maintain a unified front. Help child maintain positive peer relationships by becoming more flexible with visitations. Be a good role model in relationships and responsibilities. Continue to be the authority in your teen's life. Maintain consistent rules and standards.

Check Your Vision

1. Spend time thinking about each of your children. What are their normal developmental needs in their current stages of growth? What additional needs do each of them have because of their family situation?
2. What behaviors (if any) indicate they might need help processing some emotions?
3. Plan to spend time with each child to help meet his or her specific needs.

12

Improving Step Relationships

Grace to Let Everyone Belong

In his book *Healing Grace,* David Seamands states, "I am convinced that the basic cause of some of the most disturbing emotional/spiritual problems which trouble evangelical Christians is the failure to receive and live out God's unconditional grace, and the corresponding failure to offer that grace to others."[1] From Seamands's book, I came to understand that the opposite of living under grace is living under the oppression of performance. He compares the life of a servant (whose belongingness is based on performance) to the life of a child (whose belongingness is based on relationship):

- The servant is accepted and appreciated on the basis of what he does, the child on the basis of who he is.

179

- The servant continually worries about not pleasing his master; the child rests in the secure love of his family.
- The servant is accepted because of his workmanship; the son or daughter is accepted because of relationship.
- The servant is accepted because of his productivity and performance; the child belongs because of his position as a person.
- When a servant fails, his employment is at stake; when a child fails, it may cause grief, but he will not be thrown out.[2]

Based upon those observations, it seems that grace means belonging to someone and belonging in some place, no matter what. "Belonging" happens more naturally in an intact family than it does in a stepfamily. In an intact family the children were brought into the world by the two parents. The children literally belong to the parents and the parents to the children. The parents will always belong to each other. Nothing can be done to revoke their relatedness to each other. Correction of wrong actions and attitudes is more acceptable in intact families because no precedent has been set that one can not belong.

For stepfamilies, however, at least one parent has no blood relationship with a child. The fact that

- a child belongs only to one parent in a household;
- someone else outside the home took part in creating a child;
- a stepparent has responsibility for, but only a tenuous attachment to stepchildren; and
- the divorce set a precedent that it is possible not to belong anymore

means that stepfamilies must rely on grace for an atmosphere of belongingness to be created in their homes.

When stepchildren or stepparents do not sense that they belong, they may resort to pushing out or putting down other family members. Without grace, the threatened person will typically push back to strengthen his or her own place in the family. This cycle may go unnoticed until it has spiraled way out of control. So what can be done to help everyone feel as if he or she belongs? How should grace be received and dispensed in stepfamilies? Here are some ideas.

Foster Belongingness Spouse to Spouse

Remarried couples often feel so torn by their circumstances that marital unity and solidarity seem unattainable. That is why it is even more critical for remarried couples to make time to focus on each other, on hearing each other's hearts, and on enjoying being together. To maintain a solid, unified marriage through grace:

- Pray together regularly, casting your cares on the Lord.
- Expect your marriage to be tested, and remind each other regularly of your commitment to see it through.
- Don't allow yourself to be drawn into an unhealthy alliance with a child (or your former spouse) against your current spouse. Encourage open and honest discussions of *problems,* rather than indulging verbal assaults on *people.*
- Show kindness and fairness to your spouse's kids, even when you aren't receiving the same from them. Encourage your spouse to spend time alone with his or her children. Sincere efforts above and beyond the call of duty will speak volumes of love to your spouse.
- Schedule regular, *private* meetings (daily, weekly, or monthly, depending on the level of conflict in your

home) to *openly and calmly* discuss the state of the step-family as each spouse perceives it. Express interest in each other's point of view, and reestablish unity in dealing with each other and the children.

- Schedule regular dates. Take a break from the problems and pressures of stepfamily life. Plan opportunities to just enjoy each other.
- Build relationships with other stepcouples, both for support and for friendships.
- Attend marriage conferences to strengthen your relationship, renew your commitment, and grow in intimacy.

These are a few ways that spouses can assure each other that they "belong" even if others are trying to pull them apart.

Foster Belongingness Adult to Child

Gary Smalley and John Trent wrote a wonderful book for parents called *The Blessing*. The blessing is that sense of being unconditionally accepted and loved regardless of our successes or failures. Parents are the key people in the life of every child that either pass along that sense of blessing or leave the child longing for acceptance. "If we feel blessed, we can face life with self-confidence and joy. If we lack such a feeling, however—even subconsciously—life is full of frustration, fear, and disappointment."[3]

From their studies of the biblical blessing passed from father to son, Smalley and Trent note five elements that must be present for a sense of blessing to be imparted: meaningful touch, spoken words, expressing high value, picturing a special future, and active commitment on the part of the parent to help the blessing become a reality for the child.

Children in stepfamilies desperately need to know they are accepted and loved unconditionally. Whatever the family history has been, they need to know their future is yet to be written and has the potential for great and wonderful things. The challenge for parents and stepparents is to find ways to communicate the blessing well and often, so they may overcome their hurts and fears and impart that sense of blessing and belongingness to the children.

Imparting Acceptance to Your Own Children

Parents who do not live with their children may not have daily opportunities to communicate with them. They must, therefore, become more creative in their efforts to instill in their children a solid sense of acceptance. The following suggestions might apply whether you live with your kids or not, but they might be especially helpful for those who do not.

- Be sure they understand that the breakup of their family was not their fault. When they question the reason, be honest without being critical of the other parent, and share only things that are age-appropriate. Express your sincere sorrow over the complicated family situation that has been created for them, and let them know you are doing your best now.

- Provide meaningful touch through frequent hugs, kisses, pats, hand holding, playfully messing up their hair, a hand on the shoulder, or any other appropriate way to express affection through touch. As children get older, they may be reluctant to express affection, but they still need it from you.

- Verbally express to children their value to you, and offer words of encouragement and confidence frequently. Psychologists tell us it takes many positive messages to counteract the effect of one negative message. Terms of endearment such as positive nicknames like "sweet-heart" or "treasure" express how special your child is to you.

- When you notice them having success in a particular skill or possessing a particular positive character trait, tell them how you can see them using that skill or trait as an adult. For example, "You're so good at explaining things. You might make a great teacher someday!" Or, "You're so good at that video game! You could probably write those programs when you grow up!" Or, "You are so caring and unselfish. That's why you'll be a good mom someday."
- Spend one-on-one time both working and playing together.
- Be a good listener and perceptive of their feelings and attitudes.
- Don't allow yourself to be manipulated. Remember you are the parent first, with a responsibility to teach and train your child in healthy relationship skills.

Imparting Acceptance to Your Stepchildren

Stepparents have the difficult task of maintaining an attitude of acceptance in spite of the mood swings and possible sabotage efforts of their stepkids. Here are a few suggestions for stepparents to help stepchildren know they belong:

- Welcome the stepkids with open arms, even though they left their room in a mess the last time they came.
- Find acceptable ways to provide meaningful touch, even if it is just a light hand on the child's shoulder in passing from time to time.

- Include everyone in decision making as often as is appropriate. Take turns letting each family member have his or her preference.
- Make a stepchild's favorite foods for dinner.
- Notice and compliment changes in their features as they grow.
- Notice and compliment skills and character traits you appreciate in them.
- Refuse to compare stepchildren unfairly to your own children; don't hold them to a higher standard.
- Make sure the stepkids have a place that belongs to them in your home.
- Don't react in anger to a stepchild's attempts to hurt or undermine the marriage.
- Express love especially when a stepchild suffers a failure—failure does not cause you to lose love, respect, or status in the family.
- Forgive the trespasses of the stepkids as quickly as you forgive your biological kids or your spouse.

Foster Belongingness Child to Child

Sibling rivalry takes place in every family. In stepfamilies it becomes especially grating as wounded children from two families are forced to coexist and compete for their parents' love and attention.

I believe the underlying issues that make it a worse rivalry than in a nuclear family have to do with the children's insecurities. The burden of meeting the emotional needs of the children so that they feel more secure—like they really belong (see chapter 11, and the section "Foster Belongingness Adult to Child"

185

above)—falls on the parent. If children's emotional needs are being met well by the parents, their struggles for position and affection in the home will likely diminish.

In addition to the efforts of parents and stepparents to meet the emotional needs of all children, parents can also establish polices that may help stepsiblings better relate to each other and maybe even develop some strong attachments. Consider the following suggestions:

- Establish firm boundaries for touching or using each other's personal items. Children need to learn to share, but they also need to respect ownership of each other's items, such as toys, clothes, bedroom space, and closet space.
- Encourage older siblings to help younger ones with homework, or to read to them, or any other nurturing gesture that is age appropriate for each child.
- By your example, teach them to encourage each other and to deal kindly with each other.
- Teach them good communication and conflict resolution skills (see final sections of this chapter for suggestions on communication and conflict resolution). Allow them to work out conflicts on their own as much as possible. Don't become a rescuer or take sides in a conflict. If parents can't be drawn into a conflict, one strong motive for fighting will be quashed.

Relationship Skills 101: Toward Grace in Communication and Conflict Resolution

Most parents hope and pray that their children will avoid the relationship struggles they experienced as they matured through life. Certainly we hope they will have a better chance at a stable marriage and family life. However, we often continue modeling faulty communication patterns and weak conflict resolution skills and never teach them the skills they need to relate to us, their friends, or their future spouses and children.

Little do we realize that the more we improve in the skills of communication and conflict resolution, the better our chances of experiencing strong relationships and establishing peace in our own homes. At the same time, we are equipping our children with the skills they will need when they become adults and start their own families. Changing how we relate to others seems like a scary proposition, but knowledge is power. All relationships in your stepfamily can benefit from knowing, practicing, and teaching healthy communication patterns and biblical conflict resolution skills.

Practice and Teach Healthy Communication Skills

Family systems pioneers such as Paul Watzlawick and Virginia Satir have extensively studied the effects of communication upon the emotional well-being of children in families. Their studies have shown that good communication skills are crucial to bringing up children who relate well with others. In healthy communication, spoken messages agree in meaning with nonverbal communications such as facial expressions and other body language, as well as subsequent actions.

On the other hand, in cases where body language contradicts the spoken messages, children become unable to trust their parents. If they can't trust their parents, they become unable to trust other relationships. They may become disengaged emotionally from most relationships or so needy that they eventually drive others away.

Satir states, "One should not underestimate the importance of what the child learns from . . . misunderstandings. . . . Inadver-

187

tent learnings . . . become more powerful than any words that can be uttered."[4] Telling a child he or she is loved and important, then spoiling the relationship with the other parent (whether still married or already divorced), or missing all of the key moments of the child's development, or other similar contradictory behaviors, will contribute to such distrust.

"Inadvertent learnings" are one reason that stepfamilies should work toward healthy communications with each other. Our brains naturally enjoy putting the pieces of puzzles together. We often try to make connections where no connections exist. For example:

- *Stepdaughter:* "Why didn't my stepmom tell me she was coming home early from work? She probably wanted to see if she could catch me doing something wrong!"
- *Stepdad:* "He's being pleasant today because he wants something. Probably money."
- *Husband:* "She commented about how much the bushes have grown. I guess she wants me to get the yard work done today."

These are all examples of how people become more comfortable making assumptions about motives rather than seeking the truth in conversation. We must realize how much our assumptions hurt us.

We also need to become aware of our nonverbal messages—especially those we send unintentionally. I have learned over the past several years that I use facial expressions to say things to people that I'm too chicken to say out loud. I cast an annoyed glare at someone if I don't trust that they have told me the truth. If I disapprove or disagree with something someone said, I roll my eyes rather than get into a discussion about it. Verbally, I might say I'm open to discussion, but my body language shuts the discussion down.

Eighty to ninety percent of our communication takes place nonverbally, whether we're aware of it or not. That is why we must be sure that what we say with our bodies agrees with what we say in words. When our teenagers say that nothing is wrong yet their eyes shoot daggers into our brains, we will hear the nonverbal message ("I hate you!") much louder than the spoken message ("Nothing is wrong."). In such cases we are put into an awkward position. Which message do we respond to, the verbal message or the nonverbal one?

From Sarah Trenholm's book *Thinking through Communication*, here are some healthy communication habits to practice with your family members and to teach to your children:

- Listen empathetically. Make it your goal to understand what it is like to *be* the other person. Don't interrupt.
- Focus on relevant details.
- Control your emotions.
- Provide helpful feedback. The most helpful feedback is to paraphrase what the person has shared to show that you understood. It helps others feel heard and prompts them to think through the dilemma them-selves. Other types of feedback are giving advice, giving your analysis of their situation, giving reassur-ance and support, and questioning or probing. These methods can be useful if the other person is open or has asked for advice or an opinion. More often, they create defensiveness.
- Be careful about interpreting nonverbal cues. To really understand nonverbal messages you can:

  Consider the context of the situation. For example, if your son's arms are crossed as he talks to you, he might be angry or he might be just cold.
  Consider the other person's usual behavior. For

189

example, is your stepdaughter normally bouncy and hyperactive when asking permission to do something? If not, there might be another meaning behind the nonverbal behavior to investigate.
Ask for verbal clarification.

- Help one another become aware of unintentional messages sent through body language. [5]

Trenholm describes the three destructive communication patterns to avoid in yourself, and you can teach your children to avoid them as well.

Disconfirmation messages are responses that tell the other person that he or she is not worth our time or trouble. They include ignoring the other person, interrupting the other person, giving an irrelevant response (one that has nothing to do with the present conversation), impersonal responses that express our lack of comfort with the other person, and incongruous responses when our body language doesn't match what we say.

Paradoxes are manipulations that cause the other person to be confused about what we really want. For example, "I'm happy you get to go play golf. I don't mind being stuck at home. Alone. Again."

A *double bind* is a serious paradox in which there is no right choice. Controlling personalities often place people in double binds. For example, a stepmom might complain that her stepson doesn't help around the house, but whenever he tries, she criticizes and belittles him for doing it wrong. Both choices get him into trouble with her. [6]

Relationships are developed through communication. Without healthy communication skills, healthy stepfamily relationships cannot develop. Humbly evaluate and improve your own patterns of communication, and be a part of teaching your children healthy relationship skills for their future.

Practice and Teach Biblical Conflict Resolution Skills

To mishandle conflict is to mishandle relationships. In times of conflict we reveal what is most important to us—our desires or our relationships. All of our favorite novels, movies, and television shows base their stories around a conflict. Something that must be overcome stands between the protagonist and a goal.

I think of such movies as *Schindler's List* and *Mr. Holland's Opus.* In each of them, the hero's objective was initially self-serving. For each, a deep personal crisis forced their hearts open to the fact that their lives had a profound significance that neither wealth nor fame could provide. In the struggle to lay down their selfish ambitions, they each discovered the fullness of the human experience, and they make us want to experience it as well. We love the stories—until the story is our own life, our own conflict.

As in these movies, typically nothing is inherently wrong with our desires or goals. However, our goals often become more important to us than the people we affect by trying to reach them. A toddler who wants to play with a certain toy does not consider the feelings of the other child already playing with the toy. A stepdad who wants that position of authority in his home makes rigid rules that serve to damage relationship with his stepkids, ruining any chance of having a positive impact on their lives.

At the heart of biblical conflict resolution is the truth that we all must be willing to sacrifice our personal agendas for the benefit of a greater plan. That plan is summed up in the two greatest commands in Scripture, found in Matthew 22:36–40:

> "Teacher, which is the greatest commandment in the Law?"
>
> Jesus replied: "'Love the Lord your God with all your heart and with all your soul and with all your mind.' This is the first and greatest commandment. And the second is like it: 'Love your neighbor as yourself.' All the Law and the Prophets hang on these two commandments."

Loving God and loving others are at the heart of biblical conflict resolution. This is what we need to learn, practice, and teach our children.

In his book *Peacemaking for Families,* Ken Sande discusses three ways that conflict can be handled. One is all about "me." It is an escape strategy that may involve denial, running away from the problem, or (at the extreme) suicide. At the opposite pole is the second method that is all about "you." It is an attack strategy that may involve assault (verbal or physical), lawsuits, or (at the extreme) murder.[7] The third way of responding is all about "us." It is a peacemaking strategy. It includes the following biblical responses:

First, consider this question: "How can I glorify God in this situation?" (1 Peter 2:12). Sande states, "Our emotions—which can often be our own worst enemy—are brought under control when we focus on trusting, obeying, and imitating God."[8]

Second, determine how you have contributed to the conflict and what you should do about it. Identify goals that have become idols, realize how others have been wronged by seeking them, then confess them and repent of them. In Matthew 7:4–5, Jesus states:

> How can you say to your brother, "Let me take the speck out of your eye," when all the time there is a plank in your own eye? You hypocrite, first take the plank out of your own eye, and then you will see clearly to remove the speck from your brother's eye.

Third, determine the severity of the offenses of others against you, and if necessary, go and show the offender his or her fault. Overlook the sins that are petty (Prov. 19:11). If too serious to overlook, take steps to discuss, negotiate, or seek counseling to resolve the conflict (Matt. 18:15–17). A sin is too serious to overlook if it dishonors God, has damaged the relationship, or has harmed or may harm others or the offender.

Fourth, be reconciled (Matt. 5:23). Forgive the offender, and encourage a helpful solution to the problem.[9]

We often fear dealing with conflict because it requires us to look in the mirror and see our own selfishness. Perfect love, however, casts out all fear. Resolving conflict biblically has been a difficult process for me to learn. When I follow God's plan for seeking forgiveness from others (even if I don't feel I was in the wrong), I experience an overwhelming release and peace and a fresh closeness with God that otherwise I do not have. Yet each time I must go through the process, it is just as hard as the time before. It is always an act of obedience in faith.[10]

By working to resolve conflicts in our stepfamilies, we demonstrate our desire for each person to belong and feel accepted and to know the fullness of the human experience. God, by his grace, stubbornly refused to let us break relationship with him. In the same way, our efforts to love each other through conflict—to sacrifice our own agendas for the good of the family—extend an irrefutable grace.

Even as some people reject the grace of God unto salvation, some family members will reject the dispensation of grace in the stepfamily. But only at the point of death does God's offer cease. Never stop offering that unmerited invitation to belong.

Check Your Vision

1. Which of your family members do not have a strong sense that they truly belong in your stepfamily? What specific actions can you take to help them feel more a part?
2. In what areas of communication are you strongest? In what areas are you weakest? Choose one weak area to practice and improve on this week.
3. List the members of your stepfamily below, including yourself. Beside each name, record the style of conflict resolution you perceive each person uses the most: escape

(i.e., denial, avoidance), attack (i.e., escalation, blaming, accusing, slandering, physical aggression), or peacemaking (i.e., overlooking offenses, discussion, negotiation, seeking forgiveness, seeking to glorify God).

4. How can you begin to teach a biblical style of conflict resolution to your children?

13

Hope for the Journey

Life can seem tough on many fronts, and stepfamily life is one of the difficult situations of life. Culture's views of stepfamily life seem to make it optional—as if it is no real tragedy if a stepfamily falls apart. In reality, stepfamily life is another of the *many* important fronts in which God wants to use his people to contend for the lives of others and to reveal his love and righteousness. The commitments to serve God on the foreign mission field, in one's community or workplace, or as a parent in an intact family are no more holy than a commitment to serving God in a stepfamily. So when the going gets tough . . .

Hold on to Hope

Hope is an intangible concept, so the phrase "hold on to hope" seems an oxymoron. Nonetheless, hope is crucial. Webster's defines *hope* as a "desire with expectation of attainment."[1] Scripture uses the word *hope* to define faith: "Faith is being sure of what we *hope* for" (Heb. 11:1, emphasis added). Proverbs 13:12 acknowledges that we can maintain hope even through sadness: "Hope deferred makes the heart sick." Romans 5:2–5 demonstrates the significance of hope in a believer's life:

> And we rejoice in the hope of the glory of God. Not only so, but we also rejoice in our sufferings, because we know that suffering produces perseverance; perseverance, character; and character, hope. And hope does not disappoint us, because God has poured out his love into our hearts by the Holy Spirit whom he has given us.

Hope Comes from Persevering

In the Romans 5 passage, perseverance through suffering builds character in a believer. Character gives rise to a patient hope, a hope that looks for God's hand in everything, no matter how the situation looks on the surface.

The words *despair, desperation,* and *despondency* are used by Webster's to define the opposite of hope (hopelessness). Taking Paul's train of thought the other direction, if we do not persevere through suffering, character does not develop, and desperation, despair, and/or despondency will rule our actions (rather than a calm desire for, and expectancy of, positive outcomes).

When we try to run from suffering, we cling to false hope that we can make everything work without having to suffer. False hopes may lead to desperate acts that fail to accomplish or satisfy the real desire. Or they may lead to an apathetic acceptance of bad circumstances, and we take no responsibility to make improvements. So persevering through difficult times seems to be a key to generating true hope, and hope in turn helps one persevere through the next trial.

Hope Comes from God

According to Psalm 62:5–6 and many other passages in Scripture, the most reliable form of hope is that which comes from and is placed in God (emphasis added):

> Find rest, O my soul, in God alone;
> *my hope comes from him.*
> He alone is my rock and my salvation;
> he is my fortress, I will not be shaken.

Hope that finds its source in the Word of God is hope that won't be shaken or lead to disappointment.

Hope Comes from Stories of Others Who Persevered

Hope also comes from knowing the positive outcomes of others in similar circumstances. An article, "My Other Mother," by Sherry Boardman tells the story of her relationship with her stepmother.

Initially, as she grew up, she never really considered her stepmom a part of her life. But as an adult, after the death of her own mother, she began to visit her father more frequently and renewed her acquaintance with her stepmother. She began to confide in her stepmom, and through their talks, she gained insight to help her in her own struggles and learned that her stepmom "was a real person" with sufferings of her own.[2]

She concludes her article by stating:

Although no one can ever really take the place of the mother I've lost and the love I had for her, there is a special place in my heart for this woman, and a closeness one rarely understands without experiencing it. . . . She is [no longer] the "lady" my father married, but the person I regard, and acclaim highly and without reservation, as . . . my other mother.[3]

197

Parents and stepparents can hold on to that elusive, intangible thing called "hope" by persevering through struggles, by searching God's Word for his promises, and by seeking out the stories of others that provide concrete evidence that truly "in all things God works for the good of those who love him, who have been called according to his purpose" (Rom. 8:28). Hold on to hope.

Strengthen Resolve

The loyalty conflicts and the playing of one parent against another that occur often in stepfamilies don't just chip away at a parent's resolve to "train up a child in the way he should go." Rather they blast it away like dynamite.

Resolve can crumble in an instant when a child makes one parent feel that he or she is less fair or reasonable than the other parent. Doubting oneself, doubting one's faith, shifting focus from the character development of the child to the immediate happiness of the child, fearing once and for all losing a child's love, feeling misunderstood—all of these thoughts and feelings bombard a parent who has just carried out a difficult decision for the ultimate good of the child.

In *The Screwtape Letters* by C. S. Lewis, a master demon writes letters to a demon-in-training on how to sabotage the resolve of a new believer. The general approach of the demons is to take something good created by God (to whom Screwtape refers to as "the Enemy") and cause it to become a perverted obsession with the believer. On the subject of "The Same Old Thing" in a believer's life, Screwtape writes to his protégé Wormwood:

> The Enemy loves platitudes. Of a proposed course of action He wants men, so far as I can see, to ask very simple questions: is it righteous? is it prudent? is it possible? Now, if we can keep men asking: "Is it in accordance with the general movement of our time? Is it progressive or reactionary? Is this the way that His-

tory is going?" they will neglect the relevant questions. And the questions they *do* ask are of course, unanswerable; for they do not know the future, and what the future will be depends very largely on just those choices which they now invoke the future to help them to make. As a result, while their minds are buzzing in this vacuum, we have the better chance to slip in and bend them to the action *we* have decided on.[4]

That is the dilemma of the divorced parent and the stepparent. The questions of their hearts so easily focus on making up for the past mistakes and making everything all better. The questions they should be asking for the *true* benefit of their children are, Is it righteous? Is it true? Does it build character? Is it loving in the true sense of the word *love* (rather than the enabling sense)? By asking the relevant questions, parents and stepparents can maintain a strong resolve to carry out their responsibilities to the next generation.

Jesus demonstrated resolve on what he knew would be his final journey to Jerusalem. Luke 9:51 says, "As the time approached for him to be taken up to heaven, Jesus *resolutely* set off for Jerusalem" (emphasis added). The prophecy of this moment in Christ's life, found in Isaiah 50:7 (NKJV), describes it this way:

> For the Lord GOD will help Me;
> Therefore I will not be disgraced;
> Therefore I have set My face like a flint,
> And I know that I will not be ashamed.

The ultimate purpose for which Jesus had come to earth, to die a torturous death on behalf of the world, was quickly approaching. Jesus rebuked any attempt to deter him from what he had come to do. When Peter would not accept that Jesus would be killed, Jesus said, "Get behind me, Satan!" (Matt. 16:21–23). When the disciples tried to fight the soldiers who came to arrest Jesus, he commanded, "No more of this!" (Luke 22:49–51).

For parents of children of divorce to stay focused on the task, they must recognize the voices that seek to distract them and immediately cast those thoughts aside. They must say, "No more of this!" Hebrews 12:1–3 states it well:

> Therefore, since we are surrounded by such a great cloud of witnesses, let us throw off everything that hinders and the sin that so easily entangles, and let us run with perseverance the race marked out for us. Let us fix our eyes on Jesus, the author and perfecter of our faith, who for the joy set before him endured the cross, scorning its shame, and sat down at the right hand of the throne of God. Consider him who endured such opposition from sinful men, so that you will not grow weary and lose heart.

Accept Adversity and Work within It

America has almost always been "a land of equal opportunity." America began as a country that had to fight hard for freedom from tyranny. Later on, America fought against herself to establish that indeed all men are created equal. In the ongoing struggle to overcome evil against humanity, America more and more becomes that land where anyone can achieve the American dream.

Many of our ancestors scraped and saved to establish homes and provide for their families. However, Americans as individuals have become so accustomed to comfort that adversity is typically seen as an unwelcome anomaly, rather than a fact of daily life, and an enemy that must be obliterated, rather than a chance for growth and strength training. That attitude is found often in families, particularly in stepfamilies, and that attitude is the reason we break so easily.

Resistance Training

In the world of bodybuilding, those ugly, gear-laden weight machines were developed as a healthy alternative to barbells.

They call it "resistance training." By working through the machines in a weight room, one can, over time, strengthen just about every muscle in the body. Resisting the weight of the plates causes muscle tissue to break down during the workout. Over the next few days, the tissue rebuilds itself and comes back stronger and able to handle more weight the next time around. Repeating this process with consistency keeps one's muscles toned, rather than allowing them to atrophy.

In the same way, stepfamilies can use adversity to develop strength and resiliency. Instead of seeing adversity as an opportunity for strength training, stepfamilies often perceive it to be a battle that someone must win and someone must lose. Knee-jerk reactions cause the family muscles to rip and become permanently damaged. If parents and stepparents, husbands and wives, would instead give calm, confident, and consistent attention to areas of family conflict—not to quash the conflict, but to learn and grow through it—everyone would benefit from the process.

One area of adversity our family has experienced is what I call "the worldview wars." I know that adolescents must discover and choose their own values and beliefs. Still, my ego took a hefty blow when my stepdaughters began veering off the path we hoped they would travel. While I cannot claim we did not have some episodes of hurtful knee-jerk reactions, we've also learned to gently influence them toward godly living. Gravity wants us to come down hard on them. Resistance keeps us loving them through their discovery process and offering them a proven alternative.

Paul in the Midst of Adversity

The early apostles provide wonderful examples of working in the midst of adversity—using it as a platform to teach others. Paul and Silas remained in prison when the earthquake opened the prison doors and loosed their chains. As a result, a jailer and his family became believers (Acts 16:25–34). When Paul was arrested in Jerusalem in the midst of an angry mob, he asked to address the mob and was able to tell the story of his conversion. The crowd rejected his message, but the commotion aroused curiosity in an official who brought him before the Jewish religious leaders. Paul spent over two years in prison, all the while writing letters to churches and going before various officials to tell of his faith in Christ, ultimately to present his famous argument before King Agrippa (Acts 21–26).

Many lives changed and still change today because Paul used adversity for his own purposes. Many lives can change in families by taking advantage of moments of conflict, rather than hurriedly trying to end them.

Let Jesus Change You

Some of the godliest people I know have been through some of the most horrific life tragedies. Being put in a place where a Christian's own answers are insufficient to solve a dilemma causes a greater reliance upon God. Turning to God means seeking the most God-honoring course to take through prayer, Scripture reading, and trustworthy counsel. It also means overcoming our fear of seeing how our own attitudes sometimes throw gasoline on the fires in our lives.

Allowing the self to be transformed is possibly the most difficult of all Christian challenges. In *Mere Christianity*, C. S. Lewis likens a believer's resistance to sanctification to being an "Obstinate Toy Soldier." He states:

> The natural life in each of us is something self-centered, something that wants to be petted and admired, to take advantage of other lives, to exploit the whole universe. And especially it wants to be left to itself: to keep well away from anything better or stronger or higher than it, anything that might make it feel small. It is afraid of the light and air of the spiritual world, just as

people who have been brought up to be dirty are afraid of a bath. And in a sense it is quite right. It knows that if the spiritual life gets hold of it, all its self-centeredness and self-will are going to be killed and it is ready to fight tooth and nail to avoid that.[5]

Like the toy soldier that fears being made "real," members of stepfamilies also cling to their own ways of coping that protect their feelings and identities and keep others at a safe distance. But what if God wants to correct all of that so that they can become more and more each day like a real family instead of a toy family?

If parents of Christian stepfamilies believe the promises of Romans 8:28–29 ("all things work for good") and of 2 Corinthians 3:18 (believers are being transformed into Christlikeness), then they must also believe that God is using their stepfamily circumstances to create his Son's image in them. What an awesome thought! Rather than moaning and groaning over trials and kids, tensions and conflicts, ex-wives and child support, *ad infinitum,* parents can cooperate with the Spirit and celebrate the fact of their "ever-increasing glory, which comes from the Lord, who is the Spirit" (2 Cor. 3:18).

Anne Bradstreet, a Puritan poet who lived in the 1600s, wrote a poem called "The Flesh and the Spirit" describing the argument that takes place as the old sin nature contends with the new. I conclude with a segment from this poem, because I believe that the impact of Christian stepfamily life will be shaped heavily by that battle between the old nature of a Christian parent (or stepparent) and the new. The Spirit makes this rebuttal to the Flesh:

> Be still thou unregenerate part,
> Disturb no more my settled heart,
> For I have vowed (and so will do)
> Thee as a foe still to pursue.
> And combat with thee will and must,
> Until I see thee laid in th' dust.

Sisters we are, yea, twins we be,
Yet deadly feud 'twixt thee and me;
For from one father are we not,
Thou by old Adam wast begot,
But my arise is from above,
Whence my dear Father I do love.
Thou speak'st me fair, but hate'st me sore,
Thy flattering shows I'll trust no more.
How oft thy slave, hast thou me made,
When I believed what thou hast said,
And never had more cause of woe
Than when I did what thou bad'st do.
I'll stop mine ears at these thy charms,
And count them for my deadly harms.
Thy sinful pleasures I do hate,
Thy riches are to me no bait,
Thine honours do, nor will I love;
For my ambition lies above.[6]

May your visions and ambitions for your stepfamily lie above, and may each member be transformed into his image, from glory to glory!

Notes

Chapter 1: *Stepping In*

1. Archibald D. Hart, *Helping Children Survive Divorce* (Dallas: Word, 1996), xii.

2. Ibid., xiii.

3. *Stepfamily Fact Sheet*, Stepfamily Association of America, 28 May 2003, http://saafamilies.org/faqs/index.htm, (14 October 2003).

4. Jan Larson, "Understanding Stepfamilies," *American Demographics* 14, no. 7 (1992): 360.

5. *U.S. Divorce Statistics*, Divorce Magazine.com, 2000, http://www.divorcemag.com/statistics/statsUS.shtml, (14 October 2003).

6. *Births, Marriages, Divorces and Deaths Provisional Data for 1998*, National Vital Statistics Reports from the Centers for Disease Control and Prevention National Center for Health Statistics, 6 July 1999, http://www.cdc.gov/nchs/data/nvsr/nvsr47/nvs47_21.pdf, (14 October 2003).

7. James H. Bray, "From Marriage to Remarriage and Beyond: Findings from the Developmental Issues in Stepfamilies Research Project," in *Coping with Divorce, Single Parenting, and Re-marriage: A Risk and Resiliency Perspective,* ed. E. Mavis Hetherington (Mahwah, N.J.: Lawrence Erlbaum Associates, 1999), 253.

8. Judith Wallerstein, Julia Lewis, and Sandra Blakeslee, *The Unexpected Legacy of Divorce: A Twenty-Five Year Landmark Study* (New York: Brunner/Mazel, 2000), xxiii–xxv.

9. Paul Amato, "Children of Divorced Parents as Young Adults," in *Coping with Divorce, Single Parenting, and Re-marriage,* ed. E. Mavis Hetherington (Mahwah, N.J.: Lawrence Erlbaum Associates, 1999), 154.

10. Ibid., 159.

11. Ibid., 160.

12. Terry Teachout, "Is Tony Soprano Today's Ward Cleaver?" *New York Times,* 15 September 2002, sec. 4 , p. 3.

Chapter 2: *What Happened to "Happily Ever After"?*

1. *Merriam-Webster's Collegiate Dictionary,* 10th ed., s.v. "companion," "companionship."

2. Diana R. Garland, "Divorce and the Church," *Review and Expositor: The Journal of the Faculty of the Southern Baptist Theological Seminary* (Fall 1995): 422.

3. Sidney Callahan, "The Psychology of Family Relationships," in *The Family,* ed. Lisa Sowle Cahill and Dietmar Mieth (London: SCM Press, 1995), 27.

4. Charles Reid, "The History of the Family," in *The Family,* ed. Lisa Sowle Cahill and Dietmar Mieth (London: SCM Press, 1995), 10–11.

5. Ibid., 12.

6. Mary Ann Mason, Arlene Skolnick, and Stephen Sugarman, *All Our Families: New Policies for a New Century: A Report of the Berkeley Family Forum* (New York: Oxford University Press, 1998), 4.

7. Ibid., 12.

Chapter 3: *Breaking the Cycle of Divorce and Remarriage*

1. "Americans Identify What They Want Out of Life," Barna Research Group, 26 April 2000, http://www.barna.org/cgi-bin/MainTrends.asp, (14 October 2003).

2. "Born Again Adults Less Likely to Co-Habit, Just as Likely to Divorce," Barna Research Group, 6 August 2001, http://www.barna.org/cgi-bin/MainTrends.asp, (14 October 2003).

3. William R. Beer, *American Stepfamilies* (New Brunswick, N.J.: Transaction Publishers, 1992), xii, 28.

4. Wallerstein, Lewis, and Blakeslee, *Unexpected Legacy of Divorce*, 26.

5. *Making Marriage Last*, The American Academy of Matrimonial Lawyers, n.d., http://www.aaml.org/Marriage_Last/MarriageLastText.htm, (14 October 2003).

6. "Net Cited as Marriage Wrecker," *BBC News*, 15 April 2002, http://news.bbc.co.uk/1/low/sci/tech/1931035.stm, (14 October 2003).

7. Garland, "Divorce and the Church," 426.

8. Ibid.

Chapter 4: *The High Call of Parenting*

1. *Merriam-Webster's Collegiate Dictionary*, 10th ed., s.v. "parent."

2. "What Kids Say," Struggling Teens Discussion Forum, online posting last accessed 13 January 2001, http://www.strugglingteens.com/cgi_bin/ultimatebb.cgi?ubb=get_topic&f-4&f=000054.

3. Lionel A. Hunt, *Handbook of Children's Evangelism* (Chicago: Moody, 1960), 38.

4. Caralee J. Adams, "A Time of Compassion," *Better Homes and Gardens*, December 1999.

Chapter 5: *God Uses Imperfect Families*

1. Barbara LeBey, *Family Estrangements* (Atlanta: Longstreet Press, 2001), 50–55.

2. Ibid., 55.

3. Kenneth E. Bailey, "The Pursuing Father," *Christianity Today*, 26 October 1998, 34–40.

Chapter 6: *The Normal Stepfamily*

1. *Merriam-Webster's Collegiate Dictionary*, 10th ed., s.v. "fused."

2. Ibid.

3. *Merriam-Webster's Collegiate Dictionary,* 10th ed., s.v. "tectonic."

4. Wallerstein, Lewis, and Blakeslee, *Unexpected Legacy of Divorce,* 61–62.

5. Bray, "From Marriage to Remarriage and Beyond," 265.

6. Ibid., 261.

7. Mark A. Fine, Marilyn Coleman, and Lawrence Ganong, "A Social Constructionist Multi-method Approach to Understanding the Stepparent Role," in *Coping with Divorce, Single Parenting, and Re-marriage,* ed. E. Mavis Hetherington (Mahwah, N.J.: Lawrence Erlbaum Associates, 1999), 274.

8. Ron L. Deal, *The Smart Stepfamily* (Minneapolis: Bethany, 2002), 90–91.

9. Hart, *Helping Children Survive Divorce,* 114, 170.

Chapter 7: *Weeds from the Past*

1. *Merriam Webster's Collegiate Dictionary,* 10th ed., s.v. "bitter."

2. Paul Morrell, *Living in the Lion's Den: How to Cope with Life's Stresses* (Nashville: Abingdon, 1992), 87.

3. Neil T. Anderson, *Victory over the Darkness: Realizing the Power of Your Identity in Christ* (Ventura, Calif.: Regal, 1990), 199.

4. Ibid., 203.

5. Ibid., 203–5.

6. Charles R. Solomon, *The Rejection Syndrome* (Wheaton: Tyndale House, 1982), 85.

7. Ibid., 87–90.

8. *The 24–Hour Counselor,* "I Feel Really Guilty," recording and CD-Rom (Nashville: Broadman & Holman, 1999), found in Word-Search Bible Study software (NavPress Software).

9. David Seamands, *Healing Grace* (Wheaton: Victor, 1988), 127.

10. Ibid., 130.

Chapter 8: *Weed Killer #1: Cooperative Parenting*

1. Wallerstein, Lewis, and Blakeslee, *Unexpected Legacy of Divorce,* 10.

2. Beer, *American Stepfamilies*, 34–35.

3. Melinda Blau, *Families Apart: Ten Keys to Successful Co-parenting* (New York: G. P. Putnam's Sons, 1993), 23.

4. Donald T. Sapsonek, "A Guide to Decisions about Joint Custody: The Needs of Children of Divorce," in *Joint Custody and Shared Parenting*, ed. Jay Folberg (New York: Guilford, 1991), 30.

5. Joan Kelly, "Developing and Implementing Post-Divorce Parenting Plans," in *Nonresidential Parenting: New Vistas in Family Living*, ed. Charlene E. Depner and James H. Bray (Newbury Park, Calif.: Sage, 1993), 147.

6. Eleanor E. Maccoby, Charlene E. Depner, and Robert H. Mnookin, "Custody of Children Following Divorce," in *Impact of Divorce, Single Parenting, and Stepparenting on Children*, ed. E. Mavis Hetherington and Josephine D. Arasteh (Hillsdale, N.J.: Lawrence Erlbaum Associates, 1988), 95.

7. Wallerstein, Lewis, and Blakeslee, *Unexpected Legacy of Divorce*, 26.

8. *Merriam-Webster's Collegiate Dictionary*, 10th ed., s.v. "team."

9. Nancy S. and William D. Palmer with Kay Marshall Strom, *The Family Puzzle* (Colorado Springs: Pinion, 1996), 178–79.

Chapter 9: *Weed Killer #2: Proactive Stepparenting*

1. Kay Pasley, Marilyn Ihinger-Tallman, and Amy Lofquist, "Remarriage and Stepfamilies: Making Progress in Understanding," in *Stepparenting: Issues in Theory, Research, and Practice*, ed. Kay Pasley and Marilyn Ihinger-Tallman (Westport, Conn.: Greenwood, 1994), 7.

2. Irene Levin, "The Stepparent Role from a Gender Perspective," in *Stepfamilies: History, Research, and Policy*, ed. Irene Levin and Marvin B. Sussman (New York: Haworth, 1997), 188.

3. Beer, *American Stepfamilies*, 85.

4. Eulalee Brand, W. Glenn Clingempeel, and Kathryn Bowen Woodward, "Family Relationships and Children's Psychological Adjustment in Stepmother and Stepfather Families," in *Impact of Divorce, Single Parenting, and Stepparenting on Children*, ed. E. Mavis Hetherington and Josephine D. Arasteh (Hillsdale, N.J.: Lawrence Erlbaum Associates, 1988), 316.

5. Ibid., 318.

6. Barbara Vinnick and Susan Lanspery, "Cinderella's Sequel: Stepmothers' Long-Term Relationships with Adult Children," *Journal of Comparative Family Studies* 31, no. 3 (2000): 377–84.

7. Brand, Clingempeel, and Woodward, "Family Relationships," 300.

8. Beer, *American Stepfamilies*, 85.

9. Brand, Clingempeele, and Woodward, "Family Relationships," 320.

10. Steve and Dena Sposato, *Fruits of the Spirit: The Stepfamily Spiritual Journey* (n.p.: Stepfamily Living, 2002), 8.

11. *Merriam-Webster's Collegiate Dictionary*, 10th ed., s.v. "empathy."

Chapter 10: *Weed Killer #3: Constructive Discipline*

1. *Merriam-Webster's Collegiate Dictionary*, 10th ed., s.v. "discipline."

2. Maxine Marsolini, *Blended Families* (Chicago: Moody, 2000), 151.

3. Jane B. Brooks, *The Process of Parenting*, 4th ed. (Mountain View, Calif.: Mayfield, 1996), 41, 211.

4. Ibid.

5. Ibid.

6. Deal, *The Smart Stepfamily*, 151.

7. Ibid., 134.

8. Dick Dunn, *New Faces in the Frame* (Nashville: LifeWay, 1997), 169–70.

Chapter 11: *Emotional Fortification for Kids*

1. Brooks, *Process of Parenting*, 243.

2. David Goodman, *A Parent's Guide to the Emotional Needs of Children*, rev. ed. (New York: Hawthorn, 1969), 20.

3. Ibid.

4. Ruth P. Arent, *Parenting Children in Unstable Times* (Golden, Colo.: Fulcrum, 1993), 51.

5. Neil Kalter, *Growing Up with Divorce: Helping Your Child Avoid Immediate and Later Emotional Problems* (New York: Free Press, 1990), 310.

6. Emily B. Visher and John S. Visher, *How to Win as a Stepfamily* (New York: Brunner/Mazel, 1991), 167.

7. This chapter is intended to help parents and stepparents begin to imagine the emotional deficiencies that might exist for their children. It is not intended to present the scope of developmental needs of children. To gain a more complete understanding of this topic, the sources used in this chapter would be beneficial to readers.

Chapter 12: *Improving Step Relationships*

1. David Seamands, *Healing Grace* (Wheaton: Victor, 1988), 14.

2. Ibid., 23.

3. Gary Smalley and John Trent, Ph.D., *The Blessing* Study Guide (Colorado Springs: NavPress, 1988), 7.

4. Virginia Satir, James Stachowiak, and Harvey A. Taschman, *Helping Families to Change* (New York: Jason Aronson, 1977), 101.

5. Sarah Trenholm, *Thinking through Communication,* 2nd ed. (Boston: Allyn and Bacon, 1999), 61–65, 143–45, 176–77.

6. Ibid., 160–62.

7. Ken Sande with Tom Raabe, *Peacemaking for Families* (Wheaton: Tyndale House, 2002), 7–11.

8. Ibid., 36.

9. Ibid., 199–202.

10. For further discussion on resolving conflict, Sande's book offers extensive help in how to go about each of these steps in detail.

Chapter 13: *Hope for the Journey*

1. *Merriam-Webster's Collegiate Dictionary,* 10th ed., s.v. "hope."

2. Sherry Boardman, "My Other Mother," *Stepfamilies Quarterly* (fall 1990), http://www.saafamilies.org/education/articles/sm/boardman.htm, (14 October 2003).

3. Ibid.

4. C. S. Lewis, *The Screwtape Letters* (New York: Macmillan, 1946), 129–30.

5. C. S. Lewis, *Mere Christianity* (1952; first paperback edition, New York: Collier Books, Macmillan, 1960), 154–57.

6. Anne Bradstreet, "The Flesh and the Spirit," in *The Treasury of American Poetry,* comp. Nancy Sullivan (New York: Barnes and Noble, 1978).

Bibliography

Adams, Caralee J. "A Time of Compassion." *Better Homes and Gardens,* December 1999.

Amato, Paul. "Children of Divorced Parents as Young Adults." In *Coping with Divorce, Single Parenting, and Re-marriage.* Edited by E. Mavis Hetherington. Mahwah, N.J.: Lawrence Erlbaum Associates, 1999.

American Academy of Matrimonial Lawyers. *Making Marriage Last.* n.d. http://www.aaml.org/Marriage_Last/MarriageLastText.htm.

Anderson, Neil T. *Victory Over the Darkness: Realizing the Power of Your Identity in Christ.* Ventura, Calif.: Regal, 1990.

Arent, Ruth P. *Parenting Children in Unstable Times.* Golden, Colo.: Fulcrum, 1993.

Bailey, Kenneth E. "The Pursuing Father." *Christianity Today,* 26 October 1998: 34–40.

Barna Research Group, Ltd. "Americans Identify What They Want Out of Life." 26 April 2000. http://www.barna.org/cgi-bin/MainTrends.asp.

———. "Born Again Adults Less Likely to Co-Habit, Just as Likely to Divorce." 6 August 2001. http://www.barna.org/cgi-bin/MainTrends.asp.

BBC News. "Net Cited as Marriage Wrecker." 15 April 2002. http://news.bbc.co.uk/1/hi/sci/tech/1931035.stm.

Beer, William R. *American Stepfamilies*. New Brunswick, N.J.: Transaction, 1992.

Blau, Melinda. *Families Apart: Ten Keys to Successful Co-parenting*. New York: G. P. Putnam's Sons, 1993.

Boardman, Sherry. "My Other Mother." *Stepfamilies Quarterly,* fall 1990. http://www.saafamilies.org/education/articles/sm/boardman.htm.

Bonhoeffer, Dietrich. *Ethics*. Paperback ed. New York: MacMillan, 1965.

Bradstreet, Anne. "The Flesh and the Spirit." In *The Treasury of American Poetry*. Compiled by Nancy Sullivan. New York: Barnes and Noble, 1978.

Brand, Eulalee, W. Glenn Clingempeel, and Kathryn Bowen Woodward, "Family Relationships and Children's Psychological Adjustment in Stepmother and Stepfather Families." In *Impact of Divorce, Single Parenting, and Stepparenting on Children*. Edited by E. Mavis Hetherington and Josephine D. Arasteh. Hillsdale, N.J.: Lawrence Erlbaum Associates, 1988.

Bray, James H. "From Marriage to Remarriage and Beyond: Findings from the Developmental Issues in Stepfamilies Research Project." In *Coping with Divorce, Single Parenting, and Re-marriage: A Risk and Resiliency Perspective*. Edited by E. Mavis Hetherington. Mahwah, N.J.: Lawrence Erlbaum Associates, 1999.

Brooks, Jane B. *The Process of Parenting*. 4th ed. Mountain View, Calif.: Mayfield, 1996.

Callahan, Sidney. "The Psychology of Family Relationships." In *The Family*. Edited by Lisa Sowle Cahill and Dietmar Mieth. London: SCM Press, 1995.

Deal, Ron L. *The Smart Stepfamily*. Minneapolis: Bethany, 2002.

Divorce Magazine.com. *U.S. Divorce Statistics*. http://www.divorcemag.com/statistics/statsUS.shtml.

Dunn, Dick. *New Faces in the Frame*. Nashville: LifeWay, 1997.

Fine, Mark A., Marilyn Coleman, and Lawrence Ganong. "A Social Constructionist Multi-method Approach to Understanding the Stepparent Role." In *Coping with Divorce, Single*

Parenting, and Re-marriage. Edited by E. Mavis Hethering-ton. Mahwah, N.J.: Lawrence Erlbaum Associates, 1999.

Garland, Diana R. "Divorce and the Church." *Review and Expositor: The Journal of the Faculty of the Southern Baptist Theological Seminary,* fall 1995.

Goodman, David. *A Parent's Guide to the Emotional Needs of Children,* rev. ed. New York: Hawthorn, 1969.

Hart, Archibald D. *Helping Children Survive Divorce.* Dallas: Word, 1996.

Hunt, Lionel A. *Handbook of Children's Evangelism.* Chicago: Moody, 1960.

Kalter, Neil. *Growing Up with Divorce: Helping Your Child Avoid Immediate and Later Emotional Problems.* New York: Free Press, 1990.

Kelly, Joan. "Developing and Implementing Post-Divorce Parenting Plans." In *Nonresidential Parenting: New Vistas in Family Living.* Edited by Charlene E. Depner and James H. Bray. Newbury Park, Calif.: Sage, 1993.

Larson, Jan. "Understanding Stepfamilies." *American Demographics* 14, no. 7 (1992): 360.

LeBey, Barbara. *Family Estrangements.* Atlanta: Longstreet Press, 2001.

Levin, Irene. "The Stepparent Role from a Gender Perspective." In *Stepfamilies: History, Research, and Policy.* Edited by Irene Levin and Marvin B. Sussman. New York: Haworth, 1997.

Lewis, C. S. *Mere Christianity.* First paperback ed. New York: Collier Books, Macmillan, 1960.

——. *The Screwtape Letters.* New York: Macmillan, 1946.

Maccoby, Eleanor E., Charlene E. Depner, and Robert H. Mnookin. "Custody of Children Following Divorce." In *Impact of Divorce, Single Parenting, and Stepparenting on Children.* Edited by E. Mavis Hetherington and Josephine D. Arasteh. Hillsdale, N.J.: Lawrence Erlbaum Associates, 1988.

Marsolini, Maxine. *Blended Families.* Chicago: Moody, 2000.

Mason, Mary Ann, Arlene Skolnick, and Stephen Sugarman. *All Our Families: New Policies for a New Century: A Report of the Berkeley Family Forum.* New York: Oxford University Press, 1998.

Morrell, Paul. *Living in the Lion's Den: How to Cope with Life's Stresses.* Nashville: Abingdon, 1992.

National Vital Statistics Reports from the Centers for Disease Control and Prevention National Center for Health Statistics. *Births, Marriages, Divorces and Deaths Provisional Data for 1998.* 6 July 1999. http://www.cdc.gov/nchs/data/nvsr/nvsr47/nvs47_21.pdf.

Palmer, Nancy S. and William D. with Kay Marshall Strom. *The Family Puzzle.* Colorado Springs: Pinion, 1996.

Pasley, Kay, Marilyn Ihinger-Tallman, and Amy Lofquist. "Remarriage and Stepfamilies: Making Progress in Understanding." In *Stepparenting: Issues in Theory, Research, and Practice.* Edited by Kay Pasley and Marilyn Ihinger-Tallman. Westport, Conn.: Greenwood, 1994.

Peterson, Eugene H. *The Message.* Colorado Springs: NavPress, 1993.

Reid, Charles. "The History of the Family." In *The Family.* Edited by Lisa Sowle Cahill and Dietmar Mieth. London: SCM Press, 1995.

Sande, Ken, with Tom Raabe. *Peacemaking for Families.* Wheaton: Tyndale House, 2002.

Sapsonek, Donald T. "A Guide to Decisions about Joint Custody: The Needs of Children of Divorce." *Joint Custody and Shared Parenting.* Edited by Jay Folberg. New York: Guilford, 1991.

Satir, Virginia, James Stachowiak, and Harvey A. Taschman. *Helping Families to Change.* New York: Jason Aronson, 1975.

Seamands, David. *Healing Grace.* Wheaton: Victor, 1988.

Smalley, Gary, and John Trent, Ph.D. *The Blessing Study Guide.* Colorado Springs: NavPress, 1988.

Solomon, Charles R. *The Rejection Syndrome.* Wheaton: Tyndale House, 1982.

Sposato, Steve and Dena. *Fruits of the Spirit: The Stepfamily Spiritual Journey.* Stepfamily Living, 2002.

Stepfamily Association of America. *Stepfamily Fact Sheet.* 10 June 2000. http://www.saafamilies.org/faqs/index.htm.

Struggling Teens Discussion Forum. "What Kids Say." Online posting last accessed 13 January 2001. http://www.strugglingteens.com/cgi_bin/ultimatebb.cgi?ubb=get_topic&f-4&f=000054.

Teachout, Terry. "Is Tony Soprano Today's Ward Cleaver?" *New York Times,* 15 September 2002.

Trenholm, Sarah. *Thinking through Communication.* 2d ed. Boston: Allyn and Bacon, 1999.

24–Hour Counselor, The. "I Feel Really Guilty." Nashville: Broadman & Holman, 1999; found in WordSearch Bible Study Software, NavPress Software.

Vinnick, Barbara, and Susan Lanspery. "Cinderella's Sequel: Stepmothers' Long-Term Relationships with Adult Children." *Journal of Comparative Family Studies* 31, no. 3 (2000): 377–84.

Visher, Emily B., and John S. Visher. *How to Win as a Stepfamily.* New York: Brunner/Mazel, 1991.

Wallerstein, Judith, Julia Lewis, and Sandra Blakeslee. *The Unexpected Legacy of Divorce: A Twenty-Five Year Landmark Study.* New York: Hyperion, 2000.

Recommended Resources by Topic

Christian Resources on Stepfamily Life

Deal, Ron L. *The Smart Stepfamily*. Minneapolis: Bethany, 2002.

Dunn, Dick. *New Faces in the Frame*. Nashville: LifeWay, 1997.

Marsolini, Maxine. *Blended Families*. Chicago: Moody, 2000.

Palmer, Nancy S. and William D. with Kay Marshall Strom. *The Family Puzzle*. Colorado Springs: Pinion, 1996.

Sposato, Steve and Dena. *Fruits of the Spirit: The Stepfamily Spiritual Journey*. N.p.: Stepfamily Living, 2002.

Successful Stepfamilies. http://www.successfulstepfamilies.com.

Family and Stepfamily Research

Beer, William R. *American Stepfamilies*. New Brunswick, N.J.: Transaction, 1992.

Hetherington, E. Mavis., ed. *Coping with Divorce, Single Parenting, and Re-marriage*. Mahwah, N.J.: Lawrence Erlbaum Associates, 1988.

LeBey, Barbara. *Family Estrangements*. Atlanta: Longstreet, 2001.

Stepfamily Association of America. Stepfamily statistics. http://saafamilies.org.

Visher, Emily B., and John S. Visher. *How to Win as a Stepfamily*. New York: Brunner/Mazel, 1991.

Parenting and Stepparenting

Arent, Ruth P. *Parenting Children in Unstable Times*. Golden, Colo.: Fulcrum, 1993.

Blau, Melinda. *Families Apart: Ten Keys to Successful Co-parenting*. New York: G. P. Putnam's Sons, 1993.

Brooks, Jane B. *The Process of Parenting*. 4th ed. Mountain View, Calif.: Mayfield, 1996.

Hart, Archibald D. *Helping Children Survive Divorce*. Dallas: Word, 1996.

Kalter, Neil. *Growing Up with Divorce: Helping Your Child Avoid Immediate and Later Emotional Problems*. New York: Free Press, 1990.

Smalley, Gary, and John Trent, Ph.D. *The Blessing* Study Guide. Colorado Springs: NavPress, 1988.

Marriage and Divorce

Barna Research Group, Ltd. "Born Again Adults Less Likely to Co-Habit, Just as Likely to Divorce." http://www.barna.org/cgi-bin/MainTrends.asp. 2001.

Barna Research Group, Ltd. "Americans Identify What They Want Out of Life." http://www.barna.org/cgi-bin/MainTrends.asp. 2000.

Garland, Diana R. "Divorce and the Church." *Review and Expositor*. Fall 1995: 419–33.

Markman, Howard J., Scott M. Stanley, and Susan L. Blumberg. *Fighting for Your Marriage*. San Francisco: Jossey-Bass, 2001.

Wallerstein, Judith, Julia Lewis, and Sandra Blakeslee. *The Unexpected Legacy of Divorce: A Twenty-Five Year Landmark Study.* New York: Hyperion, 2000.

Inspiration, Spiritual Growth, and Healing

Anderson, Neil T. *Victory Over the Darkness: Realizing the Power of Your Identity in Christ.* Ventura, Calif.: Regal, 1990.

Bonhoeffer, Dietrich. *Letters and Papers from Prison.* New York: Macmillan, 1953.

———. *The Cost of Discipleship.* Rev. and unabridged ed. New York: Macmillan, 1968.

Lewis, C. S. *Mere Christianity.* New York: Collier Books, Macmillan, 1960.

———. *The Screwtape Letters.* New York: Macmillan, 1946.

Peterson, Eugene H. *The Message.* Colorado Springs: NavPress, 1993.

Seamands, David. *Healing Grace.* Wheaton: Victor Books, 1988.

Solomon, Charles R. *The Rejection Syndrome.* Wheaton: Tyndale House, 1982.

Communication and Conflict Resolution

Sande, Ken, with Tom Raabe. *Peacemaking for Families.* Wheaton: Tyndale House, 2002.

Satir, Virginia, James Stachowiak, and Harvey A. Taschman. *Helping Families to Change.* New York: Jason Aronson, 1975.

Trenholm, Sarah. *Thinking through Communication.* 2d ed. Boston: Allyn and Bacon, 1999.

Kay Adkins has been a stepmom for over thirteen years. She holds an M.A. in communication from Southwestern Baptist Theological Seminary and is a freelance writer, with articles published in *Discipleship Journal* and the *Baptist Press*. She also teaches Sunday school and writes curriculum for children's programs. She and her husband, Carl, live in Mountain View, Arkansas.